FLIPPING THE SWITCH
OF THE
CREATIVE POWER
OF YOUR
SUBCONSCIOUS MIND

BY FREDRICK MOORE
COPYRIGHT © 2015 MOORE PUBLISHING LLC

All Rights Reserved. This book was printed in the United States of America. No part of this book may be used or reproduced, transmitted, or stored in any manner whatsoever without express written permission in advance from the author, except for brief quotations for review purpose only.

Moore Publishing, LLC
P.O. Box 1883
Cedar Hill TX 75104
www.moorepublishing.com
www.moorepublishing.net
www.flippingtheswitch.net

ISBN: 978-1-5136-3149-3

ACKNOWLEDGEMENT

This book was written at the sole discretion of the author. These views and opinions are the views and opinions of the author. This book was written to teach, encourage, motivate, and inspire the reader to change their habitual thoughts, for the changing of their lives. By practicing the principles and creative process discussed in this book, I hope for the reader to begin utilizing their creative thoughts and ideas for the progression of their lives. My hope is for the reader to understand and realize how creative and powerful their thoughts and ideas truly are. These principles, the creative process, and method of thinking is not my invention, creation, or original ideas. They have been around since the beginning of time. My writings have been highly influenced by the likes of Thomas Troward, Ralph Waldo Emerson, and James Allen to name a few. But my greatest influences are the teachings of the Bible, Jesus Christ, and my Oneness with God. My hope is for the reader to understand their power within and begin to create a life that is pleasurable, enjoyable, and desirable for themselves.

    I would like to dedicate these writings to my beautiful daughters A'jah and Jayla Moore. You two are the pride, joy, and inspiration of my life. You both motivate me to be better and to do better. I now understand the unconditional love a parent has for their children.

    To my parents Freddie and Sharlene Moore, thank you both for being the example of authentic love. You guys have taught me the true meaning of real sacrifice for others, through the love and support you have given to me.

To my former wife and friend Tanya Moore, thank you for your support and raising my beautiful, intelligent, wealthy minded daughters. Thank you for allowing and accepting me to be my true self, while co-parenting with you. Our girls are a true resemblance of us both mentally and spiritually, and I am very grateful for that. But thank God, they have your beauty.

To my brother Johnathan, and sisters Mylene, Catherine, and Carrie. Thank you for all your love and support. My relationship with each of you is different, but very special.

To my cousin Jeanetta Brown thank you for blessing me with such a beautiful book cover. You brought my vision to life and I am very grateful for that.

I Love All of You Guys Very Much!

Table of Contents

ACKNOWLEDGEMENT 3
PREFACE 7
INTRODUCTION: NEW THOUGHT 13
SECTION I 19
UNDERSTANDING THE POWER YOU HAVE WITHIN 21
YOUR CONSCIOUS AND SUBCONSCIOUS MIND .. 27
UNDERSTANDING YOUR SUBCONSCIOUS MIND 33
STEPS TO UTILIZING YOUR SUBCONSCIOUS MIND 41
VISION BOARDS 53
CREATING WEALTH AND YOUR SUBCONSCIOUS MIND 57
LET ME SAY THIS 65
SECTION II 69
CAUSE AND EFFECT 71
CRABS IN A BUCKET SYNDROME 77
JEALOUSY, ANGER, AND ENVY 85
FEAR AND DOUBT 95
THE POWER OF FORGIVENESS 101
DEFINING YOUR RELATIONSHIPS 107

HAVING SELF-CONFIDENCE 113

CLEARING YOUR LINES OF COMMUNICATION 121

LET ME SAY THIS 127

SECTION III 131

BEING THANKFUL, SHOWING GRATITUDE, AND ENCOURAGING OTHERS 133

YOU HAVE POWER IN YOUR THOUGHTS 141

OUR LIMITLESS POWER OF THOUGHT 147

THE EVOLUTION OF THOUGHT AND EMOTION 155

THE UTILIZATION OF WILL POWER 163

LOVE, FAITH, AND HOPE 169

CREATING GENERATIONAL BLESSINGS 175

LET ME SAY THIS 185

BONUS 191

A MESSAGE FROM THE AUTHOR 193

PREFACE

IT IS A MAN'S OWN MIND, NOT HIS ENEMY OR FOE, THAT LURES HIM TO EVIL WAYS.

-BUDDHA

PREFACE

I wrote this book to bring awareness to the individual about their power within. I want to inform the reader about the power of their thoughts. I begin gaining this knowledge several years ago and utilized the process to enhance and enrich my life. The problem is, after experiencing a little success I begin to lean unto my own understanding. Feeling as if I was the source and the reason that these great things were starting to happen for me. I felt the little that I knew was enough and I did not need to gain any more knowledge. Besides I was the one making things happen for me, per my perceptions.

I started to lose focus, my thoughts begin to be all over the place, my faith begin to fade, and my life begin to be in turmoil. The real estate market crashed, and my entire livelihood was gone. I became bitter, my thoughts and emotions were entirely negative. I was a complete emotional mess. As if things could not get any worse, the Federal Government knocks on my door and informs me that I was being indicted. At that moment, not only did I feel like I had lost my mind, but I felt my life was over.

I begin to justify and make excuses for all my business practices. I felt like the entire world was against me. I begin to play the victim role, not willing to take responsibility for anything that had happened in my life. I started to dig myself into a deeper emotional hole. I tried to camouflage all my problems with the use of marijuana and alcohol. But when I would sober up, my problems were still there. My relationships became dysfunctional, I felt myself pulling away from the people I loved.

One day while I was packing up my things preparing myself for prison. I ran across a few books of mine that I had read a while back. I begin to reminisce when I first read these books, and how focused I was during the time I started reading them. As I begin to open them up and flick through the pages I started reading some of the passages. I begin to think about what my life would have been like if I had continued implementing the things I was learning from these books.

Once I was incarcerated I became overwhelmed but had to learn and adjust to the different personalities, different attitudes, different emotions, and different mood swings of other inmates. I remember saying to myself "I'm different," "I don't belong here," and "how could I do this to myself." But I had to deal with it, so I decided to be productive with my time. I started visiting the library and I ran across a book, that was like the books I had started studying at home. This book along with the ones I was familiar with all focused on your thoughts, the law of attraction, and your subjective or subconscious mind.

The books I had at home could not be found, so I reordered them, had them sent in to me, and I started studying them. My thoughts begin to change, and I became more open-minded to my situation. I made a conscious decision to myself that I was going to learn from my mistakes and not let my mistakes dictate my life. So, I started being more considerate of others, I treated people the way I wanted to be treated. I controlled my thoughts and emotions not letting inmates, correction officers, or the conditions I was in dictate my behavior. I began to accept my present moment for what it was. Focusing my thoughts on the way I wanted things to be, as if they already were.

But as I became more aware of things, I could not help but to recognize all the negative thoughts, emotions, ideas, and conversations that would take place around me every day. That is when it hit me. When I first came to prison I felt I was so different, but now when I look back at my behavior before coming to prison. I begin to recognize the one thing I had in common with every drug dealer, embezzler, bank robber, etc. Our thinking was the same, we all had irrational and fallacious thoughts. It was our thinking, our thoughts that had created the conditions, circumstances, and surroundings we were living in. The only real difference now about them and me was that my thinking had changed. Once I realized this, it gave me a better understanding of the people I was incarcerated with.

I had to understand first how we were alike and correct that, before any real change could begin to take place in my life. The more I began to study and understand about the creative power of our subconscious mind, the more I begin to understand why so many of us live every day with undesirable conditions, circumstances, and surroundings. I had to first understand why my life was so undesirable before I could understand anyone else's undesirable life. *"You hypocrite, first take the plank out of your own eye, and then you will see clearly to remove the speck from your brother's eye." Matthew 7:5*

So, this is just what I have done. I now understand how my thoughts had created an undesirable life for me, and I have learned from my mistakes. Knowing the things, I know now, I wish to share this information with anyone who wants to understand. I want to inform everyone, how to flip the switch of the creative power of your subconscious mind. I would like to share with you some priceless information about our thought process that will change your life forever.

The one thing about prison, is that I have had the chance to sit back and collect my thoughts and reflect on my life. I have had the chance to examine and gain understanding, as to where I went wrong in life, but most importantly, how not to make those mistakes again. I have had a chance to rehabilitate my mind. I have pushed a restart button that has cleared my mind and allowed me to restore it with some life changing information about our thought process.

I now understand the power of our thoughts, and the creative abilities of our thoughts. I now understand how our thoughts have always dictated our lives since the beginning of time. I now understand how our conscious and subconscious mind work. But most importantly how to make them work for me. I now know how to flip the switch of the creative power of your subconscious mind. and I would like to share this priceless information with you.

INTRODUCTION: NEW THOUGHT

THE CREATIVE PROCESS BRINGS THE MATERIAL AND CONDITIONS FOR THE WORK TO OUR HANDS; THEN WE MUST MAKE USE OF THEM WITH DILIGENCE AND COMMON SENSE- GOD WILL PROVIDE THE FOOD, BUT HE WILL NOT COOK THE DINNER.

-THOMAS TROWARD

INTRODUCTION: NEW THOUGHT

When I speak of the words new thought I am not speaking of a specific movement, religion, or church. I am speaking of a method of thinking that is the inherent element by which the development of our lives is brought about. It is the utilization of our thoughts, emotions, and beliefs being in harmonious unification to bring forth our desires through the creative power of our subconscious mind. It is the individual specialization of universal law for the creative process. These principles may present to the reader a new way of thinking, but this method of thinking is not new. It has existed before the creation of the world.

They are the comprehensive and fundamental doctrine of the Creative Spirit Itself, God. The principles themselves are not new because principles are universal and infinite. But it is the acknowledgement and utilization of these principles that will begin producing new results in our lives because we begin to exercise them. It is the working of these new-found principles in our lives that begin to shine a new light on our thoughts and our mental state. We need to understand that our thoughts have creative power. We were created in the image and likeness of God. It is for this reason we must never forget that our Creator has given us the power to create in the world He has created.

Our minds were created in the image and likeness of God's Mind and we were created for the Spirit of God to enjoy life in us and through us. Our recognition of the creative power of our thoughts must be consciously in harmonious agreement to the ideal of our relation to God. We are never separated from God; any misunderstanding of a separation is due to our ignorance of the inherent relations between us and God. When our conscious mind receives a thought or desire that is perceived as true, because it is in harmonious agreement with our emotions and beliefs, it impresses that thought onto our subconscious mind. Our subconscious mind is the creative mind. It is One with the Creative Source Itself, God. It does not judge our desires, it creates what the conscious mind tells it to.

Our subconscious mind is our line of communication with God's Mind. God's Mind is Infinite Intelligence. Our subconscious mind represents the individual, it has its own individuality. It is the individual selfhood that differentiates one individual from another. It is the "I am this because I am not that." But because we can acknowledge the individuality of ourselves and others, it communicates the idea of limitation. We confirm through our recognitions of individuality where our individuality begins and ends.

God's Mind has no self-acknowledgement of individuality. If It recognized within Itself a place where something begins and ends, It could not be acknowledge as God. Because for something to have a beginning and an end implies limitation. God's Mind is Infinite Intelligence, It is exhaustless, limitless, and knows the answer to all, because It created all. For God's Mind to acknowledge anything as being beyond Itself would be a rejection of Its own existence.

God's Mind do not have individuality It has personalness*. This inherent personalness[1] of the Divine is in all that exist. Now let's understand there is a difference between individuality and personalness. The word individuality relates to a person's character, their characteristics. It is commonly coupled with the word

---

[1] *Thomas Troward-The Edinburg Lectures on Mental Science Receptivity

personality. When I speak about the word personalness, I am referring to the personal quality of God's Mind beyond individuality.

Now we must comprehend that the Spirit of God passes through all space and essential nature. It passes through us mentally and spiritually and all existing things. This means that all persons or things are filled by an inner personalness, limitless in its possibilities of intelligence, responsiveness, and power of expression, waiting to be brought into action by our acknowledgement of it. But it will only respond to us according to our recognition of it. Our recognition of it is through our thoughts, emotions, and beliefs. It is through our thoughts, emotions, and beliefs of our relationship with God that we call this limitless power into action. The personalness of God's Mind is the Source of all individual personalities. It answers or replies in its highest expression to those who acknowledges its personal essence.

Our recognition and acknowledgement of the limitless power of God's Mind, always being in perfect harmony and unity with our subconscious mind, allows us to create conditions, circumstances, and surroundings with infinite instructions and power. It is the individual mind, the subconscious mind that receives its power, guidance, and strength from the Infinite Intelligence and Wisdom of the Supreme Mind, God's Mind, and it allows the subconscious mind to create. It is our faith and belief in this Oneness and the connections of these two minds that allows us to create and direct our lives with certainty by impressing our desires upon the subconscious mind for the betterment of our lives. This is what I am speaking of when I say you have power in your thoughts, because this process works whether you are aware of it or not.

What we must comprehend is, we are giving direction willingly or unwillingly to our mind. Our mind is limitless, and it creates. Since God's Mind do not have personality, we are able to impress upon It our own personality and influence It with our own personal desires through our subconscious mind. The Intelligence and Impersonality of God's Minds enables It to receive the impressions of our thoughts through our subconscious mind, and It also directs our subconscious mind to the best and simplest way of accomplishing our desires. Now this is the functioning of our minds.

When we let our negative conditions, circumstances, and surroundings of poverty and lack dictate our thinking, our negative emotions move into harmonious agreement with our negative thoughts and beliefs producing more situations of poverty and lack. It is the recognition and comprehension of this process that allows us to make our subconscious mind work in our favor by directing our thoughts, emotions, and beliefs in a positive direction. We must have unwavering faith and belief of its supreme achievement of our desires.

God's Mind is impersonal therefore It has no concerns or judgements of the desires of the individual and neither does the subconscious mind. The fact that It is impersonal means that It has no intentions. This creative power of our subconscious mind moves and creates at the direction of our conscious mind, according to our habitual thoughts, emotions, and beliefs.

SECTION I

UNDERSTANDING THE POWER YOU HAVE WITHIN

A MAN IS WHAT HE THINKS ABOUT ALL DAY LONG.

-RALPH WALDO EMERSON

22

UNDERSTANDING THE POWER YOU HAVE WITHIN YOU

The power we have inside of us is limitless. Each of us have the power and ability to change the world. The sad thing about this is, most of us go through life not knowing about this power we have within us. Hoping and wishing that something will change for us. While most of us have just given up on life and has accepted the poverty we were born into. We go through life miserable wondering why we have so little, and others have so much. Not recognizing the power, we have within ourselves to better our lives.

We move through life faithless and hopeless. The one thing that is truly disturbing, is that we pass these beliefs of not being able to be, and not being able to do onto our children. Creating a curse that last generation after generation. Fear and doubt has ruled over our lives and communities for decades. We have become afraid of opportunity, and our low self-esteem leads us to believe we are born a failure.

We think negative thoughts about every situation. We say discouraging things to ourselves like "that's a dumb idea." "that will never work," "I don't want to make a fool out of myself," and "people might think I'm dumb." It is this way of thinking that has caused people to fail throughout their entire life. It is this way of thinking that deflates any confidence a person may start to develop. It is this way of thinking that has demagnetized the blessings in our lives that is necessary for our growth and success.

We go through life everyday not knowing that we have the power inside of us to change these things. It is like walking into a home every day sitting in the dark, because you believe the power does not work. When all you have to do is flip the switch. Well today I hope to get you to flip the switch and turn on the light you have inside of you and stop living in the dark.

    This switch we need to flip ignites the creative power of our subconscious mind from negative to positive. To start this process, we must begin to change our thought process and the way we think. You can attract everything you desire in life to live abundantly. By utilizing the creative power of your subconscious mind, you become a magnet drawing to you the things and people you want and need in your life. Begin to live a joyful life full of peace, love, joy, and happiness. Begin to create the wealth, health, and prosperity you want for yourself and your family. Begin to create generational blessing for your children and grandchildren.

    Through the creative power of your subconscious mind you have the infinite intelligence within you to show you everything and anything you need to know. You begin to acquire a knowledge of information that helps you to create new ideas and thoughts, if you remain open-minded and receptive. The creative power of your subconscious mind has the wisdom to attract to you the right business, associates, or mate. It can produce all the money you need and create the financial freedom your heart desires. Your subconscious mind can find solutions to every problem you may encounter.

    By utilizing this power of your mind, you start to live a life of abundance and love. I know this power works, because I have experienced it firsthand. There is nothing like this magnificent power. It can heal souls, mend hearts, and open minds alike. We all are blessed with this power and after reading this book, I hope you start to utilize your power within and flip the switch of the creative power of your subconscious mind.

YOUR CONSCIOUS AND SUBCONSCIOUS MIND

YOUR LIFE IS WHAT YOUR THOUGHTS MAKE IT.

-MARCUS AURELIUS

YOUR CONSCIOUS AND SUBCONSCIOUS MIND

To comprehend this process, we must understand that we have only one mind, and all our minds work the same. Our mind has the power of two different characteristics or functions. These two functions of the mind operate differently, but each is furnished with its own unique qualities and powers. The names to describe the two functions of our mind is the objective and subjective mind, also commonly called the conscious and subconscious mind. You can view them as voluntary and involuntary mind, or the outer and inner mind. But we will refer to them as the conscious and subconscious mind throughout this book.

The creative power of your subconscious mind is a comprehensive and fundamental law. It is a Divine Principle and works correspondingly to the law of belief. According to Webster's Dictionary, belief is a state or habit of mind in which trust or confidence is placed; something believed. Belief is the law of the mind. The thoughts that regulate your mind. Your subconscious mind responds to your thoughts. It responds to the things you think about the most, because those are the things you believe in your own mind, your habitual thoughts.

Everyday people thoughts are concentrated on their conditions, circumstances, and surroundings of poverty and the belief of not having. Not realizing that these experiences is just the response of their subconscious mind to their thoughts. People dwell on being poor, so their habitual thoughts are focused on being poor. People stress over not paying their bills, so their habitual thoughts are focused on their bills not being paid. Leading to them remaining in poverty and their bills not being paid.

People look at their surroundings and the beliefs of not being able to be, not being able to do, and not being able to have, gets implanted into their thoughts. So, the only thing that gets reproduce in their lives is not being able to be, not being able to do, and not being able to have, because these are the seeds (negative thoughts) of life that they are sowing into their subconscious mind. You can begin now to change this process and sow seeds (positive thoughts) of peace, love, success, abundance, prosperity, and wealth. Do not let your conditions dictate the way you think. For every thought we have, there is a cause and every condition are its effect. Therefore, it is extremely important that we take charge of our thoughts so that we can start to have the conditions that we desire.

When we start to change the way we think, the creative power of our subconscious mind will respond and start to create conditions, circumstances, and surroundings that is in harmonious agreement with the positive thoughts we are having. By controlling the way we think, meaning our thought process, we can begin to utilize the creative power of our subconscious mind and use it to find the answers to the questions we may have about creating wealth, health, and prosperity for our lives. So many people today are living a life full of chaos, limitation, lack, and confusion. This is because their conscious mind is overloaded with fear, anger, doubt, and envy. They live their life with the belief of "It will never be me," "I'm not worthy or good enough." They live their entire life constantly creating conditions to reinforce these beliefs.

When our conscious mind rationalizes these thoughts as being the truth, because these are our habitual thoughts, emotions, and beliefs. These negative thoughts begin to manifest form in the subconscious mind, which is where the creative process of our lives take place. The subconscious mind believes, accepts, and makes true anything the conscious mind commands it to. So, by knowing this if we begin to influence the thoughts of our conscious and subconscious mind with positive thoughts, we will be able to transform our entire life. In order to change the effect (our conditions), we must first change the cause (our thoughts). We must begin to change the way we think and envision great ideas in our minds.

Vision yourself as being great, and doing great things, and great things will start to happen for you. Start living your life from the world within and not from the world without. Because from the world without is where most of us are living our lives today. Your subconscious mind is receptive to the sense impressions of your thoughts. You have all the power within you to create a life full of the limitless riches your heart desires.

Imagine your thoughts as molds of the things you desire, and these molds are filled by the Infinite Intelligence of your subconscious mind. With the information about the laws of your mind that you will receive from this book, you will start to understand that you have the power within. Begin to create wealth and prosperity instead of poverty, experience love instead of anger, and turn opportunity into success. You will begin to realize that fear cannot exist where there is love, faith, and hope. Start to experience the blessings that God intended for you, when you were created.

Stop speaking into existence the things you do not want and speak life into your heart desires. Your subconscious mind takes you literally at your habitual thoughts and puts you into a position that you can or cannot receive things depending on your beliefs. If you think you cannot afford it, then circumstances will occur to make sure you cannot afford it. When you start believing you can afford it and will have it, the subconscious mind creates a way for that thing to happen for you. It has always been this way, and it will always be this way, this process never fails. Always refrain from using negative statements such as, "I can't,", "I won't," or "I'll never." Instead use the opposite and speak in positive statements such as, "I can," "I will," or "I am able."

Create a mental picture of the things you desire in your life, accept them mentally into your thoughts. Meditate on these things repeatedly with an absolute degree of certainty, having unwavering faith, and your subconscious mind will find a way to make sure you receive it. Whatever your conscious mind believes your subconscious mind will achieve. The subconscious mind is always working every day of every minute. It does not discriminate or judge what you desire. It does not distinguish between good or bad, right or wrong. It will make provisions for your habitual thinking. When you change your habitual thoughts, you will change your life.

UNDERSTANDING YOUR SUBCONSCIOUS MIND

IF WE ARE TO BETTER THE FUTURE WE MUST DISTURB THE PRESENT.

-CATHERINE BOOTH

UNDERSTANDING YOUR SUBCONSCIOUS MIND

There are three remarkable facts regarding the subconscious mind. The subconscious mind has creative power. The subconscious mind is amenable to suggestion. The subconscious mind is in no way limited by precedent. To comprehend the creative power of the subconscious mind we must first accept the reality that this creative power is confined within us.

Thought is the only action of the mind. The first step to creating anything starts with that thing existing in the mind as a thought. It becomes recognized by the mind as something you desire. The creative power within you acknowledges these thoughts, allowing you to materialize what you desire. You think with your conscious mind and when you think with emotion, feeling, belief, conviction, and accept an idea as true, the conscious mind impresses these thoughts upon your subconscious mind.

Your conscious mind has the power to impress or change any thoughts, images, or concepts, held in the subconscious mind. The subconscious mind is the creative mind, it has the power to create, and it complies, conforms, and follows any commands given by the conscious mind. This is what I mean when I say the subconscious mind is amenable to suggestion. Because your subconscious mind does not distinguish if your thoughts are good or bad, true or false, positive or negative. It only responds and reacts to your habitual thoughts. You will always get a response or reaction from your subconscious mind, and it is determined by the thoughts and images you keep in your conscious mind. This is the law of your mind.

If you consciously believe something to be true, your subconscious mind will accept it as true because you consciously believe it as true and will begin to bring about the necessary consequences. Your subconscious mind does not reason, make comparisons or think for itself, it works on the command of the conscious mind. If you are living in poverty, fear, anger, doubt, anxiety, and undesirable conditions. This is due to your negative thoughts and beliefs impressed upon your subconscious mind. You need to influence your mental state with positive thoughts. Begin to impress images of perfect health, success, wealth, prosperity, and abundance. Develop positive emotions and feelings of belief and conviction about what you desire out of life. If you want to change your conditions, circumstances, and surroundings, know you can. All you must do is, change the way you are thinking and believe you can.

    I practice saying and writing affirmation statements to impress the thoughts and images of the things I want, onto my subconscious mind. Do not worry about how it is going to happen, just believe that it is going to happen and continue to do the work. The subconscious mind will create the how, all you need to do is continuously work toward what it is that you really want. But you have to want it, I mean have unwavering faith that this thing is already true and that it is currently happening. I will be discussing writing affirmations, meditation, and prayer, throughout this book.

    If you are a person of faith that believes in God, or a Higher Infinite Power, other than yourself. You need to comprehend with certainty that you are One with your Divine Source, and you can connect and tap into that Source at any time. For me that Source is God and I know that He has an Omnipresence in my life and He allow me to utilize the creative power of my subconscious mind. It is through the beliefs and thoughts that are impressed onto your subconscious mind that has created the life you have today. *Proverbs 23:7 states "For as he thinks in his heart so is he." Marcus Aurelius states "Very little is needed to make a happy life; it is all within yourself, in your way of thinking."*

This knowledge of the subconscious mind manifesting our beliefs and thoughts into existence has been around since the creation of man. Most successful writers, business persons, entrepreneurs, inventors, scientist, artist, etc., have profound comprehension of the functions of the subconscious mind. Your life reflects you. You are the one responsible for the results your life is receiving. You have been the writer, director, producer, and actor, in this movie of your life. The great thing about all of this is, now that you are aware of it, you also have the ability to yell "cut" and make the proper changes.

We start by rewriting the way we view ourselves and the way we think. We must direct our attention to the things we want in life, and not the things we do not want. We must produce a positive spirit within ourselves that allows our thoughts, emotions, and beliefs to remain positive. So that we are able to act out and perform the enjoyable experiences of life we desire for ourselves. But we must trust and have faith in the creative power of our subconscious mind. We have been blessed with this power and we have been using it our entire lives not realizing it. Regardless of what we believe, the laws of the universe, the laws of attraction, and the creative power of our subconscious mind are real.

They have been working since the beginning of time and will continue to work. We must start utilizing this Divine Power to create the life we desire. We must rid ourselves of negative thoughts and emotions and restore them with positive thoughts and emotions. Living a life of abundance, success, wealth, and prosperity, is your essential birthright. If you are not experiencing the life you desire, it is an indication that something is wrong. But understand this, you have the power within to transform your life and create it to be exactly the way you want it to be. Eliminate your destructive thinking, negative emotions, and acknowledge the Omnipotence of your subconscious mind. Begin to create the bliss and liberty you desire.

Another remarkable fact about our subconscious mind, is that it is not limited by precedent. The elements of time have no bearing on its actions. What this mean is, it does not matter what our past was. Our past has no effect on its creation. It does not matter what our parents had. It does not matter what our current conditions are. Our subconscious mind is creative and limitless, but we cannot tell it when, where, why, or how to bring about its effects. We must continue to do the work and remain patient for its results.

We can start right now and make a conscious decision to change our lives, by changing the way we think. We do this by changing the thoughts and images we have in our mind. We start by changing the way we think about ourselves. We must start to believe that despite our past, we are worthy to be successful and live a life of abundance. We must rid ourselves of the stinking thinking we are accustomed to.

We must believe and know that there are unlimited resources out there and stop living a life of lack, because we think there is not enough to go around. Despite our past or current situation, we must develop self-confidence within ourselves and get rid of the spirits of jealousy, anger, and envy. We must replace them with love, forgiveness, and encouragement. We must not let our past dictate our future and understand that we have the creative power within to determine the life we lead. Make an honest decision today to change your life. Make an honest decision today to change the way you think. Begin to believe in yourself and get rid of any fear and doubt about the things you are capable of accomplishing.

STEPS TO UTILIZING YOUR SUBCONSCIOUS MIND

DIGNITY CONSISTS NOT IN POSSESSING HONORS, BUT IN THE CONSCIOUSNESS, THAT WE DESERVE THEM.

-ARISTOTLE

STEP TO UTILIZING YOUR SUBCONSCIOUS MIND

When I think about how I process the things I desire to generate in my life, I break them down into three steps or phases. These steps or phases are create, visualize, and believe. Each of these steps play a vital role in the creative process for me. I will be discussing each of these steps with you. As you start to learn more about your subconscious mind and become more confident, you will begin to develop a process that is best suited for you. But I believe these steps can work for anyone that apply them.

CREATE

EVERY GREAT DREAM BEGINS WITH A DREAMER
-HARRIET TUBMAN

The power of our subconscious mind is limitless. I say this because the Divine Source that is One with our subconscious mind is limitless. So, we are capable of being, and doing anything that we desire. It is because of our ignorance that we continue to live a life of without. Lacking the knowledge of the creative power that is within us. So instead of living a life from within we live a life from without. We must first grasp the fact that the power to create is within us. Everything that was ever manifested or created started with a thought. Your thoughts create the world you live in.

When I think of the word create, words such as originate, compose, and produce come to mind. The word create means to bring into being; to produce through artistic or imaginative effort. Whatever ideas, ambitions, or desires we have, our subconscious mind is One with the Divine Source that brings them into reality. Knowing how our mind functions, we must begin by impressing positive, loving, and constructive thoughts about ourselves and the things we desire onto our subconscious mind. I do this by writing and saying affirmation statements to impress these thoughts and images onto my subconscious mind. An affirmation is a positive assertion that something is true. *"So is my word that goes out from my mouth: It will not return to me empty, but will accomplish what I desire and achieve the purpose for which I sent it." -Isaiah 55:11*

When I write my affirmations, I write them stating "I <u>My Name</u> AM." I write and say them like this, to write and say my statements in the first-person singular, of the present tense, of the verb TO BE. It is the proclamation of something that exists perfect, flawless, and complete. It affirms and acknowledges the Being within myself and my Oneness with God (the I AM), which is the Source of all individualize being. I prefer to write and say my affirmations using this format, but you can write yours and say them in a format that you feel comfortable with. But keep them in the present tense. For example:

I <u>Name</u> AM a very wealthy businessman/businesswoman.
I <u>Name</u> AM a very wealthy businessman/businesswoman.

Or

I <u>Name</u> AM a successful entrepreneur.
I <u>Name</u> AM a successful entrepreneur.

Or

I <u>Name</u> Am a great writer.
I <u>Name</u> Am a great writer.

Or

I <u>Name</u> AM healthy and well.
I <u>Name</u> Am healthy and well.

    I write and say my affirmations, as if they are currently happening. I truly believe that, because I asked for it in prayer, I have already received it, so I just continue to claim it. You can write and say your affirmations to fit whatever it is that you desire. I say my affirmations in the morning when I awake. I also say them at night before I go to bed. Another way I instill them is by writing them several times every day in a notebook, that is strictly for my affirmations. I write them about 20 times each. But again, you find what works for you. You must figure out what it is that you desire, and that is what you focus on.
    Do not focus on or write about things you do not want, and that is not in the present tense. Do not write things such as:

I <u>Name</u> hope I do not lose my job.
                                 Or
I <u>Name</u> wish I had $<u>dollar amount</u> in my bank account.
                                 Or
I <u>Name</u> hope my utilities do not get turned off.
                                 Or
I <u>Name</u> want a promotion on my job.

These things are negative and are not in the present tense. You are focusing on negative things. You are hoping that you do not lose your job, or your utilities do not get turned off. You are wishing for a dollar amount in your account.

You are wanting for a promotion. These affirmations do not breathe confidence and are not in the present tense.

You are the one that is creating what you desire, so state exactly what it is that you desire. Be clear and assertive about what it is that you desire, claim it, and your subconscious mind will see to it that you receive it. Meditation and prayer helps me also. I use meditation and prayer to nurture my spirit. They help me stay in a positive emotional state. Being in a positive emotional state helps you to benefit from the creative process. I will address these topics more in the Believe Phase of the creative process.

VISUALIZE

DO NOT DWELL IN THE PAST, DO NOT DREAM OF THE FUTURE, CONCENTRATE THE MIND ON THE PRESENT MOMENT.
                    -BUDDHA

When I think about what it means to visualize, words such as think, foresee, conceive, and imagine, comes to mind. The word visualize means, conjuring up a mental image or picture. This mental image or picture is seen clearly in the mind's eye. The mind's eye is the mental faculty of conceiving imaginary or recollected scenes. It is where your mental images and pictures are conceived. Now the visualization phase is an important step in the creative process of the subconscious mind. Once you know what it is that you desire, you should picture yourself being, or doing this in the end results. You are to imagine this and feel the excitement and joy of being and doing what your heart desire, as if it is happening now. You are to imagine this as if it is currently taking place.

Your emotional state plays a vital role in the visualization phase. So, it is very important that you feel good, confident, and positive about what it is that you desire. You cannot imagine being wealthy or successful and feel bad or discourage by your current conditions. What you imagine, and feel must agree with each other. They must be in harmony. Again, visualize what you desire and see it clearly in your mind's eye, as if it is currently happening at that moment.

This is the most productive and simplest way to compose an idea in your mind. When the idea is generated in your imagination, sustain it there as a mental image and imagine you can hear, feel, and experience whatever the circumstances, deed, act, or accomplishments are that you desire to be created by your subconscious mind. You need to feel excitement, joy, love, and happiness throughout your entire body. Your emotions should be in a positive state, as if you are experiencing whatever it is that you are visualizing. These mental images that are formed into your imagination are impressed onto your subconscious mind, because your conscious mind tells it that these are your desires. These impressions become materialized as facts and experiences in your life.

We get our subconscious mind to accept these images of thought by feeling the reality of them right now, as if these things are happening. Now understand this, you are using your imagination and feelings not will power. We need to comprehend the fact that it is not us, it is not our will power that has the creative power. But it is our subconscious mind that is One with the Divine Source, and we are utilizing the power we were given access to. We must stay out of our own way by trusting and believing that our subconscious mind knows the simplest and best way for us to achieve the life we desire to have for ourselves.

God is the only POWER behind the Creative Power, and we were also created by this Power. So, we cannot create what has created us. But because we are One with God, The Divine Source, it is through our subconscious mind that we can provide the appropriate conditions and utilize this limitless creative power for our benefit.

Take electricity for instance, we never created this power. But by providing specific conditions we can use it in a variety of useful and beneficial ways. Now take the same electricity, provide specific conditions that are not beneficial, that are not useable, and it can kill you. We never created this power, but we can personally make it work for us, or misuse it and make it work against us. These are the same capabilities of the creative power of your subconscious mind. So why not use it in a beneficial way to make it work for you. You have the capability through your subconscious mind to utilize your imagination and ideas to create the life you desire to have for yourself.

BELIEVE

GO CONFIDENTLY IN THE DIRECTION OF YOUR DREAMS. LIVE THE LIFE YOU HAVE IMAGINED.
-HENRY DAVID THOREAU

When I think about the word believe, words such as faith, accept, feel, expect and conviction comes to mind. According to the Webster's Dictionary the word believe means, to have a firm religious faith; to accept as true genuine or real; to have a firm conviction as to goodness, efficacy, or ability of something. We all in a way has formed our beliefs about certain things. When I discuss this phase of believe, I am talking about an absolute certainty of faith and belief that the thoughts and ideas, that you have created, by visualizing through your imagination will be materialized by following the guidance and direction of the creative power of your subconscious mind. You believe this, because your subconscious mind is One with the Divine Source. *"For assuredly, I say to you, who ever say to this mountain, be removed and be cast into the sea; and does not doubt in his heart, but believes that those things he says will be done, he will have whatever he says." -Mark 11:23*

Belief is the law of life. Our beliefs are the foundation of the life we have today. According to what we believe about ourselves and the world we live in. It is through our thoughts and beliefs that the conditions of our lives are established and materialized. Our lives are a product of our habitual thinking. The problem is, we continue to let our negative conditions, circumstances, and surroundings, dictate the thoughts and beliefs in our mind and soul. This negative way of thinking is continuing to leave us with undesirable results. *Mark 9:23 states "If you can believe, all things are possible to him who believes."* We can start changing the way we think by establishing a positive attitude about the things and life we have right now.

We must rid our minds of the negative and destructive images about ourselves and replace them with the positive and constructive images we desire. We must believe in the creative power of our subconscious mind and know without any doubt that this power is real and true. We must understand and acknowledge that our subconscious mind attracts to us whatever our thoughts and beliefs are. We spend our entire lives believing we are not worthy, believing we are not deserving, and believing we cannot be or do.

Knowing what you know now, why not change that belief. You can flip the switch and start believing you are worthy, believing you are deserving, and believing you can be or do whatever it is that you desire.

Meditation and Prayer are techniques that I use to help establish and strengthen my beliefs. Meditation and prayer are powerful techniques to help you establish and strengthen positive emotions throughout your mind and soul. They help to put you in a positive or feel good state of mind. The word meditate means to engage in contemplation or reflection; reflect on or ponder over; to plan or project in the mind. While the word pray means to make a request in a humble manner; to address God or a god with adoration confession, supplication, or thanksgiving. Psalms 23:1-3 is a prayer I like to meditate on quite often. I meditate on this prayer every night before I go to sleep and in the morning upon waking up. I meditate on the prayer by reflecting in my imagination what each verse means to me.

Psalms 23:1-3 states "The LORD is my shepherd; I shall not want. He makes me to lie down in green pastures; He leads me beside the still waters. He restores my Soul; He leads me in the paths of righteousness for His name's sake." This is how I break it down to reflect. *"The lord is my shepherd; I shall not want."* I look at a shepherd as being a guardian and protector. He protects the sheep from wolves, coyotes, or anything that can harm them. He tends to their needs and cares for them. He makes sure they eat and provides shelter for them. Being aware of this, it strengthens my belief in knowing that the LORD is my guardian and protector and he will provide whatever it is that I need or desire. So, I meditate on Him watching over me, protecting me, and providing anything that I need or desire.

"He makes me lie down in green pastures." I meditate on laying down in a big field full of joy, success, wealth, great health, happiness, and prosperity. *"He leads me beside the still waters."* I meditate on Him leading me to a calmness of peace and quietness to ease my mind. *"He restores my Soul."* I meditate on Him reviving my soul and renewing my spirit. Refreshing my mind, getting me ready to start a new day, putting my past behind me. *"He leads me in the path of righteousness for His name's sake."* I meditate on Him guiding and directing me to the simplest way of achieving my desires, and because I believe in Him, and know that He is my Source, I know without a doubt in my mind, He will answer all my prayers.

This is just one of many prayers I say to myself and meditate on. You can turn to Psalms for some prayers or create your own. You might find a scripture that suits you, and you may want to meditate on it to strengthen your spirit of belief. Sometimes to uplift my spirit I would just repeat at different times throughout the day and meditate on phrases such as "I can feel God's love throughout my spirit" or "My mind overflows with the peace and calmness of God." Saying these prayers throughout the day helps me to feel good, and they put me in a positive emotional state.

I say a prayer and meditate before I say or write my affirmations. I find that by doing this, it strengthens my beliefs. Because by praying and meditating, I acknowledge my spirit as being One with God. I believe by acknowledging my Oneness with God, it reinforces my belief in the creative power of my subconscious mind to materialize my affirmations and desires. Which empowers me to create a life of love, success, joy, happiness, wealth, and prosperity. The substances my soul desires. *"Be anxious for nothing but in everything by prayer and supplication, with thanksgiving, let your request be made known to God." -Philippians 4-6*

VISION BOARDS

VISION IS THE ART OF SEEING WHAT IS INVISBLE TO OTHERS.

-JOHNATHAN SWIFT

VISION BOARDS

They say seeing is believing. I believe vision boards are another creative way to assists you in being assertive to your subconscious mind, as to what it is that you really want. But first let's get a clear understanding of what this board is, and what is its purpose. When I think about the word vision, words such as think, conceive, image, visualize, and imagine comes to mind. The word vision means a thought, concept, or object formed by imagination: mode of seeing or conceiving. A vision board is a board you create, by assembling pictures of the things you want manifested and materialized in your life. The purpose of creating this board is to help you conceive a clear mental image or idea into your mind or thoughts of what it is you really want.

Here is the process for creating a vision board. First you get a poster board, a piece of card board, or you can use any type of board that you can glue, tape, staple, or fasten pictures onto. I prefer poster board or card board because you can move those items around quite easily, and you can move or place your vision board wherever you want or need to. It does not matter the color of the board. Whatever color you prefer is fine. Next get some pictures from magazines, books, or newspapers of the things you want manifested and materialized in your life

For example, if I see a picture of a car I want in a magazine, I would clip the picture of the car out of the magazine and tape or glue it onto my board. If I see a picture of my dream home in a magazine or newspaper I would clip the photo out of the magazine or newspaper and tape or glue it onto my board. It could be a stack or pile of money, an airplane, a person of influence, a vacation resort, or a person meditating for peace. Whatever it is that you desire tape or glue it onto your board until your board is complete. You can put on your board as many things as you want. It is your board, so you decide.

I would look at the items on my board every day to help me establish a clear and assertive image in my mind of what it is that I desire. By constantly viewing this board everyday throughout your day, you are creating the images of the person or things you desire to be or have into your mind. These images become clearer and clearer onto your mind assisting and supporting the create, visualize, and believe phases for utilizing your subconscious mind. Vision boards are a valuable tool to use in helping you to utilize the creative power of your subconscious mind. It helps you to strengthen your ideas, mental images, thoughts, and beliefs. It helps you to gain the mental focus needed when praying and meditating. Strengthening your belief in the creative power of your subconscious mind to materialize your desires.

By using vision boards and writing affirmations, I am creating a clear idea and mental image into my thoughts of what it is that I want. Allowing me to visualize with certainty, that this is exactly what I want. I just need to remain patient and receive it. *"Then the LORD answered me and said: Write the vision and make it plain on tablets, that he may run who reads it. For the vision is yet for an appointed time; but at the end it will speak, and it will not lie. Though it tarries, wait for it; because it will surely come it will not tarry." -Habakkuk 2:2-3*

CREATING WEALTH AND YOUR SUBCONSCIOUS MIND

MEN ARE BORN TO SUCCEED NOT FAIL.

-HENRY DAVID THOREAU

CREATING WEALTH AND YOUR SUBCONSCIOUS MIND

When I think about the word wealth, words such as fortune, riches, money, inheritance, abundance, and financial freedom comes to mind. The word wealth means abundance of valuable materials possessions or resources: abundant supply. The ability to create wealth is probably the number one topic on everyone's mind while reading this book. Most of us strive for self-improvement to be wealthy or to create wealth for our families. Creating wealth is a common goal for most of the people in this world. We feel having wealth would help us get rid of much of our problems and make our lives a great deal better.

I think being wealthy is great. Being wealthy gives us the financial freedom we desire. It allows us to create a better life not just for our children, but for generations to come. Being wealthy gives you prestige, influence, and power. It allows you to do things and go places that most of us can only dream about. People that are wealthy go to the best schools, have the best doctors, live in the best homes, and drive the best cars. Their perceptions of life are totally different from someone who is poor.

Now I know we have some pessimistic people out there who will say "wealth isn't everything," "wealth creates more problems," "wealth is the root of all evil." I got two words for them. "Think Positive!" Wealth is a product of the mind. It is not the wealth that is evil, it is what some of the people that have it, do with it.

There is a lot of great benefits from being wealthy and I will rather have wealth than to be without wealth. Wealthy people teaches their children about wealth. They teach them how to keep it and how to attain more of it. They have a different mindset about wealth. They know that they are worthy and deserving of it. It is passed down from their ancestors to generation after generation.

The poor also have a different mindset about wealth. They think it is inaccessible and unattainable. They do not know they are worthy and deserving of it. The problem is, when you grow up poor you are not taught about wealth. When you are poor, money is only discussed in the terms of lack, such as not having any or not having enough. It seems impossible to get and if you do attain a little of it you better hide it and do not tell anyone you got some.

If wealth is a product of the mind as I believe. Then it is the uppermost importance for poor people, middle class people, and people who just want a better life for themselves to flip the switch of the creative power of your subconscious mind. You must change the way you think. You must develop a newfound belief about wealth. You must realize that there is plenty of wealth to go around and that you are worthy and deserving of it. You must develop a different mindset about wealth and know that it is accessible and attainable. You must appreciate wealth and be receptive to receive it.

Once we achieve wealth we must teach our children about the benefits of wealth. We must begin to teach our children how to keep it and multiply it. We must begin to teach our children about their inner abilities and how to utilize their thoughts, ideas, and mental images to create wealth. We must teach them how to build wealth into their mentality. We must begin to teach our children about utilizing the creative power of their subconscious mind.

We must get them to understand that their subconscious mind is limitless and have a multitude of ideas to create wealth. We must teach them to rid their minds of the negative perceptions about wealth. We must empower their minds to develop positive and creative thoughts, ideas, and mental images about wealth, that will ignite the creative power of their subconscious mind to materialize their desires. Developing a subconscious certainty about wealth will cause their mind set about wealth to change and enhance their lives.

I believe the ideas impressed upon your subconscious mind about wealth, determines if you will be wealthy or have a life of poverty. I believe being wealthy is a product of your thoughts and emotions coming into agreement with your beliefs about your desires. Wealth is a positive harmonious state of mind and soul. You cannot have a conflict of the mind and soul and expect to be wealthy. The desire to have wealth with the idea and belief you can have wealth will create it. *Matthew 18:19 states "Again I say to you that if two of you agree on earth concerning anything that they ask, it will be done for them by My Father in heaven."*

When your thoughts, ideas, emotions, imagination, feelings, mental images, and beliefs agree about your desires, it will be done for you. This is what the Bible says, and it talks about only two, but we focus on a positive harmonious unification of them all. The purpose for this is to avoid any conflict of the mind and soul, and to provide you with the best opportunity to accomplish your desires. That is why it is important to keep a positive attitude and keep a positive emotional state. This helps you to strengthen your positive beliefs about the thoughts, ideas, and mental images you are impressing onto your subconscious mind.

The reason why writing and saying affirmations does not work for some people, is because they say one thing, but believes and feels a different way. They say positive things they desire to create, but they let the conditions around them, keep their emotions in a negative emotional state. They do not have any belief that their desires will come true. They let their conditions continue to dictate the outcome of their lives. Belief in your thoughts, ideas, desires, and imagination with childlike faith is the key to creating wealth by using the creative power of your subconscious mind. The idea and belief of being wealthy, creates wealth. Reinforce the idea and belief of wealth by meditating on the words success, wealth, prosperity, and abundance. Repeat these words for several minutes throughout your day and at night, impressing the idea and belief of wealth upon your subconscious mind.

Believe in the phenomenal power within your subconscious mind, and it will manifest positive conditions, circumstances, and surroundings, providing the simplest way for you to create wealth. Your subconscious mind has a limitless number of ideas to create wealth. You must believe in its magnificent power. Absorb this fact into your spirit, it is our birthright to be wealthy. We are put here to lead a life of love, joy, success, wealth, happiness, and abundance. We were created to flourish and succeed financially, mentally, and spiritually.

Our desire to be wealthy is a desire for a greater life. Wealth gives us the freedom we desire. The Wisdom of the creative power of your subconscious mind directs and guides you to the path of financial, mental, and spiritual wealth. By conveying the thoughts, ideas, mental images, and beliefs of wealth to the subconscious mind, you will always attract wealth. Acknowledging the creative power of your subconscious mind and belief in the creative power of your thoughts, ideas, mental images, and desires is the way to creating wealth. Let's focus on creating a positive mental and emotional state, and the wealth will come.

LET ME SAY THIS

The creative power of our thoughts is supported by scripture throughout the Bible. *"All things whatsoever ye pray and ask for, believe that ye have received them, and ye shall receive them" Mark 11:24.* Now some people may not read or follow the Bible and that is fine. You can still utilize the information given because your religious belief, background, ethnicity, sexual gender, etc., has no effect on the workings of the subconscious mind. It works the same no matter what. But I do read the Bible and I use the scriptures to help me and others reinforce this Divine Principle and strengthen our belief and faith.

I agree with Thomas Troward when he says "The Bible is the Book of Emancipation of Man. The emancipation of man means his deliverance from sorrow and sickness, from poverty, struggle, and uncertainty, from ignorance and limitation, and finally from death itself." We were not put here to suffer and be unhappy. We were created in the image and likeness of God. When we grasp the true significance of this, we begin to acknowledge the power He has instilled within us.

We begin to realize He has given us the ability to create our own world within the world He has created. So that the Spirit within us, may enjoy and experience life through us. You have the power and control to do the things you want to do. When we begin to use this Divine Principle all fear, doubt, and concern will begin to vanish. When we start to use our creative power within, we will begin to see with certainty that this Infinite Power responds and move at the direction of our habitual thoughts.

Now is the time to make the conscious decision to change your life. You start by getting rid of the destructive thoughts that is in your mind. This way of thinking is dysfunctional and has caused nothing but fear, doubt, anger, jealousy, and envy to rule your life. It is time to replace the habitual thinking of your subconscious mind with constructive thoughts that are positive. Thoughts that promote love, joy, optimism, forgiveness, gratitude, and happiness. You must change your attitude and start to believe you are worthy of being wealthy. You must believe that despite your past, you are able to accomplish your dreams. Buddha states "He is able who thinks he is able." Meaning if you believe you can do it and believe you are worthy, you will do it.

When we desire something, it starts with a thought. We must nourish our thoughts and keep them alive. We must envision ourselves being and doing the things we desire most. But most of all we must believe we are worthy of these things. We need to understand that it is who's we are, that is just as important as to who we are, and that it is our birthright to have a life of abundance, joy, and happiness. *"The Spirit Himself bears witness with our spirit that we are children of God, And if children, then heirs-heirs of God and joint heirs with Christ." -Romans 8:16-17*

You have the capability to change the conditions, circumstances, and surroundings, you are currently living in. But it is up to you to utilize your power that is within, so that you can stop living a life of without. You must make the conscious decision to start using the creative power of your subconscious mind to work in your favor. This power is real whether you believe it or not, and you use it every day. The difference now is that you have the knowledge to start benefiting from this power and take control of your life.

By following the steps to utilizing your subconscious mind you can begin to construct the life you desire. Writing and saying affirmations is a technique that has been effective in my life. I continue to use them every day. The subconscious mind is One with the Divine Source. It is omnificent and is always knows the best and simplest ways to accomplishing our desires. Prayer and meditation, allows you to communicate in a calm and peaceful manner with the Inner Wisdom of your subconscious mind. You can gain the strength, knowledge, and guidance you need to be prosperous in every area of your life. We pray to be thankful for the things we have and to ask for the things we desire.

When *Mark 11:24 states "What things so ever ye desire, when ye pray believe that ye receive them and ye shall have them."* This tells us that through our thoughts and beliefs, accept our desires as true, and believe that our desires have already been achieved and completed, then our desires will materialize. Because of our habitual thinking, our thoughts, the images, and convictions of our desires are already a reality in our mind. It is through our beliefs that we accept our desires as true and trust the intimate power of our subconscious mind.

Matthew 9:29 states "According to your faith let it be to you." We must truly comprehend the reality that we control our own destiny and no one else. We have been given the power to do the things we want. We were created in the image and likeness of God. When we undoubtedly comprehend what that means and believe in the limitless power He has instilled within us through our subconscious mind. We will begin to realize that we have been given the mental power to achieve and attain whatever we set our minds on. We have been given the power to create. We can accomplish whatever we desire.

SECTION II

CAUSE AND EFFECT

ALL THAT WE ARE IS THE RESULT OF WHAT WE HAVE THOUGHT. THE MIND IS EVERYTHING. WHAT WE THINK WE BECOME.

-BUDDHA

CAUSE AND EFFECT

A person is the causer of their conditions, circumstances, and surroundings. It is an enduring truth that can never be changed. For every action of cause there is its direct consequences of effect with it. We will never avoid the order of cause and effect. A person may not choose their conditions, circumstances, and surroundings directly. But we can choose our thoughts. It is our thoughts that indirectly shapes our conditions, circumstances, and surroundings. Cause and effect is perfect and keeps a true course in the unconcealed kingdom of thought.

We must begin to take control of our lives by regulating the thoughts of our mind and the emotions of our soul. We must stop placing blame on others, control our emotions, and take responsibility for our own well-being. When we do this, we will begin to utilize the regulating factors of our thoughts and emotions for the benefit of our lives. We will begin to discover and acknowledge the creative power within ourselves. We will begin to create for our lives the conditions, circumstances, and surroundings we desire. When a person consciously considers the emotional effect of their thoughts, they realize the effect their thoughts have on their life.

No thought is ever kept in secret, because there will come a time when that person is truly revealed, and their thoughts begin to present themselves as habits of that person, creating the effects of their life. A person with thoughts of fear, doubt, and worry begins to reveal themselves as confused, anxious, and cowardly. They live a life of defeat, faithlessness, and timid-ness. A person with thoughts of jealousy, anger, and envy begins to reveal themselves as resentful, malicious, and spiteful. They live a life of hate, displeasure, and violence. A person with thoughts of selfishness, entitlement, and blaming begin to reveal themselves as self-centered, stubborn, and full of excuses. They live a life only for themselves, running away from every challenging situation of their life, disappointing the people they claim to love.

Now if a person has thoughts of love, life, and beauty they begin to reveal themselves as kind, enjoyable, and loving. They live a life of happiness, healthiness, and prosperity. A person with thoughts of assurance, self-confidence, and courage begin to reveal themselves as confident, trusting, and reliable. They live a life of freedom, success, and wealth. A person with thoughts of love, faith, and hope begin to reveal themselves as selfless, caring, and encouraging. They live a life with purpose that is beneficial to the people they love.

These are the cause and effect of our lives. It is our thoughts, our way of thinking that has caused the conditions, circumstances, and surroundings in our lives that we deem to be unpleasant. When we observe all the displeasures of our environment, it has an emotional effect on us. Our outside conditions create negative emotions within us, causing our thoughts to become negative. We do everything we can to change our conditions, circumstances, and surroundings but our frustrations only multiply because no real change take place in our lives. Our frustrations strengthen our negative emotions, reinforcing the negative thoughts in our mind, creating more displeasing conditions, circumstances, and surroundings.

What we must understand is, we are fighting and revolting against an effect, when we ourselves are the creators of its cause. We will never change the outside conditions, circumstances, and surroundings until we begin to change what is on the inside. We must change our habitual thoughts and emotions, to change the messages of creation we are sending to our subconscious mind. We must first change what is on the inside before any real change can take place on the outside. Another way I like to view cause and effect is the sowing and reaping of a seed. Our thoughts are a representation of the seeds we are sowing, positive thoughts or negative thoughts, the cause. The results or the conditions, circumstances, and surroundings of our lives are a representation of what we reap, the effect.

Any gardener will tell you that whatever seed they plant, or sow is exactly what they will produce or harvest. Jesus illustrated the truth of seed sowing through his parables using facts of nature as his examples. Our thoughts, emotions, and beliefs are the statements spoken from our mind and soul, which are the seeds that we sow. It is through the sacred law of effect that our lives are the results of those things, because our lives are produced after their kind. We are what we think. The fruits of our lives or the results of our lives is a production of the seeds or thoughts of our mind that we are sowing. Our character and behavior are the development of our thoughts. Our happiness and misery are the fruits brought forth by our thoughts.

The sweetness of our fruit or our enjoyableness and agreeability for our lives, represent the positive thoughts or seeds we are sowing. The bitterness of our fruit or our displeasure and disagreeability for our lives represent the negative thoughts or seeds we are sowing. We develop outstanding character and behavior through the efforts of positive thinking. We develop disgraceful character and behavior through the efforts of negative thinking. It is our thinking that makes us who we are. Our thoughts are the maker and master of our character and behavior, the creator of our conditions, circumstances, and surroundings.

    We hold the answers to any situation within ourselves to solve any problems that develops in our lives. It is our thoughts that produces the outcome of our lives. If you are living a life that is undesirable, you must understand that you are blessed with the capabilities to change things and create for yourself a life that is desirable. The same way you have created the chaos and disorder in your life is the same way you change it, through your thoughts, emotions, and beliefs. The utilization of the creative process can change your life to be what you desire it to be. But it is you that must make the conscious decision to change the habitual thoughts of your mind to change the results you are receiving from your life.

    Once you begin receiving the results in your life that are desirable to you, share this information with others to enhance and enrich their lives. Sharing the knowledge, you possess to help others change their lives is another way of sowing seeds. Blessing others with the knowledge you have to better their lives come back to you as a product in your life, because this is the law of cause and effect. The results of your life, is what you sow. Good thoughts always produce good results. Just as a good tree will always produce good fruit. We are the sowers of what we harvest.

CRABS IN A BUCKET SYNDROME

YOU WILL NOT BE PUNISHED FOR YOUR ANGER, YOU WILL BE PUNISHED BY YOUR ANGER.

-BUDDHA

CRABS IN A BUCKET SYNDROME

When I mention having crabs in a bucket syndrome, I believe most people understand what I mean. But to make sure I am clear about the point I am making, I will explain this as thoroughly as possible. A crab is any of an infraorder with a short broad usually flattened carapace, a small abdomen that curls forward beneath the body, short antennae, and the anterior pair of limbs modified as grasping pincers. A crab is also an ill-tempered or angry person: to find fault with; criticize.

A bucket is a typically cylindrical vessel for catching, holding, or carrying liquids or solids. The word bucket also means to move about haphazardly or irresponsibly: Hustle, Hurry. The word haphazardly means marked by lack of plan, order, or direction. A syndrome is a group of signs and symptoms that occur together and characterize a particular abnormality or condition. A set of concurrent things (as emotion or actions) that usually form an identifiable pattern. A distinctive or characteristic behavior pattern.

When discussing the actions of crabs in a bucket from observing them. We will begin to talk about how they are all fitted into one bucket, climbing over each other, trying to scale the wall of the bucket to get out. When one reaches a height above the others, they are pulled back down into the bucket by the other crabs. Making sure they do not climb out of the bucket. When I talk about the crabs in a bucket syndrome that I observe in neighborhoods, households, and relationships, let me explain.

The word crab in relations to humans will be an ill-tempered or angry person. I am pretty sure each of us could name a few people, know a few people, or we ourselves personally fits this description. When I talk about the word bucket in relations to humans, I am talking about the place or places that we move about irresponsibly with a lack of plans, order, and direction for our lives. Our ghettos, neighborhoods, households, families, or relationships. When I talk about the word syndrome in relation to humans, I am talking about a set of concurrent things (as emotions and actions) that usually form an identifiable pattern. A distinctive or characteristic behavior pattern. These things could be from the conditions of how a person was raised and where they grew up, causing them to have an attitude of misery and complaint.

So, when I put this all together, I am referring to me, you, and the people in our lives that for whatever reason, are angry, mad, or irritable at the world. Because we seem to be stuck in the ghetto or a particular neighborhood, household, family, or relationship with no plans, order, or direction for our lives. Because we seem to lack everything such as education, positive role models, money, love, hope, and faith. Our lives are dictated by our past, our conditions, and our failures. We get so caught up in our own self-pity that it hurts us to see anything good happen for anyone else. We find happiness and joy in the misery and disappointments of others. The phrases "I knew they couldn't or wouldn't do it," "I told you so," and "I knew I was right" brings comfort to every part of our soul.

We do everything we can to discourage others from leaving this place of misery that we seem to have found comfort in. When we do hear of someone or know of someone trying to leave, especially if they are a close friend or a family member. We tend to get mad and angry at them for no apparent reason. Deep down inside we wish only the worst for them. We try to influence and discourage them with our words or negativity. We do any and everything we can to make it hard for them to succeed. Refusing to help them in any way possible, because jealousy, anger, and envy rules the throne of our soul.

We look forward to the day when we get to say, "I knew I was right." Pulling them back down into the misery that we dwell in. This is the crabs in the bucket syndrome I talk about. This is the disease, the disorder, the sickness, and the pathological mental condition of the mind that I am speaking of. This impairment of the mind caused by anger, fear, doubt, hopelessness, jealousy, and envy leads to this dysfunctional behavior pattern. We must recognize, confront, and abolish this mentality. This crabs in a bucket syndrome or mentality must be annihilated for the development, and progression of our thought process.

If this is our mentality, and these thoughts are the seeds we are sowing, we shouldn't be surprised of the fruit we are bearing or the lives we have made for ourselves. It is consequential that we begin to encourage one another, support one another, and help one another climb the wall of success. We must develop a mentality and thought process of "your success is my success." We must begin to be happy and celebrate the success and accomplishments of others. Rejoicing in their achievements and conquering of obstacles.

If you are reading this and you recognize this crabs in a bucket syndrome or mentality as any of your characteristic behavior patterns. Make a life changing decision right now to abolish, I mean exterminate this pathological condition of the mind, and begin to change your thoughts about the success of others. Begin to flip the switch of the creative power of your subconscious mind. Take in the knowledge you receive from this book and implement it into your life. Understand that you can no longer rejoice in the downfall and misfortunes of others. Because misery breathes envy, envy breathes jealousy, and these negative emotions love all the company they can get. So, this negativity will only breathe more negativity back into your life.

If you want a life full of growth, a life full of love, a life full of prosperity, you must begin to change the thoughts, ideas, and mental images in your mind that are causing you to have these negative emotions. By flipping the switch of our thoughts, we will begin to help, support, and encourage others, as well as rejoice in their accomplishments and success. Your life is a result of your thoughts, emotions, and beliefs, so begin to change them, and you will begin to change your behavior. You will begin to develop a behavior pattern that reflects having a positive mind and spirit that inspires and emboldens others.

If you are reading this and you recognize this crabs in a bucket syndrome or mentality as a characteristic behavior pattern of others, displayed toward you. Stay encouraged and do not allow this sick behavior of others to influence you or your decisions in any way. All you can do is control your thoughts and emotions, so you make sure you do just that. Remain supportive and encouraging toward them and any others you may experience or have experienced this behavior with. Do not allow them to anger you and cause you to develop the mentality to fight hate and anger with hate and anger. Stay true to who you are and continue to display the positive qualities and attributes of having positive thoughts and positive emotions. Do not allow them to pull you down to their level.

Be the positive influence and do what I call "sway them with your love." If you maintain love, faith, and hope within your spirit the negative vibes coming from others will never get to you. Their negative thoughts and emotions can never exist where love, faith, and hope lives. So, they will never be able to influence your life. *Proverbs 25:21-22 states "If your enemy is hungry, give him food to eat; if he is thirsty, give him water to drink. In doing this, you will heap burning coals on his head, and the LORD will reward you."* You must always do the right thing. You and only you can control your thoughts and emotions. Keep them in the right place and God will work wonders in your life.

But keep your thoughts and ideas close to your heart and do not allow others to discourage you from your desires. You cannot control the mental sickness and motives of others. But you can control how you respond. Everyone is not going to believe in you and your desires. They may criticize your thoughts, ideas, and vision, because of the lack of self-confidence they have about themselves. Do not let the limited minds of ill-tempered individuals, who cannot see beyond their past experiences, their conditions, and their failures influence or discourage the life you envision to have for yourself.

Be prepared to cut ties with people while on your way to success. You may very well have to relinquish relationships in order to allow the growth and development of your thoughts, ideas, and vision for the achievement of your success. Everyone is not going to appreciate or take positive advantage of you giving them a helping hand. But do your part and extend help to those you can help. We must rid our lives of this crabs in a bucket syndrome. Understand, you do not have to pull others down to uplift yourself. In fact, do not be afraid to push others up, because they may very well be the ones to help pull you out. But whatever happens, do not allow anyone to pull you back into the bucket, from which you came out of.

JEALOUSY, ANGER, AND ENVY

HOLDING ON TO ANGER IS LIKE GRASPING A HOT COAL WITH THE INTENT OF THROWING IT AT SOMEONE ELSE; YOU ARE THE ONE WHO GETS BURNED.

-BUDDHA

JEALOUSY, ANGER, AND ENVY

When discussing jealousy, anger, and envy, I would like to observe how these damaging emotions relate to each other. I would also like to discuss the importance of eliminating these detrimental emotions for the necessary growth and development of a positive emotional state. When I think of the word jealousy, words such as possessive, envious, suspicious, and distrustful comes to mind. The word jealousy means a jealous disposition, attitude or feeling. When a person is jealous they become resentful and envious of another individual or situation.

The emotion of jealousy is usually triggered by the emotion of fear. I say jealousy is triggered by fear because the person develops emotions of jealousy due to their loss of courage or confidence. They become fearful of being replaced by someone else in regard to another's affection or they have lost the courage and confidence to follow their dreams. So, they become jealous of others causing feelings of bitterness, apprehension, and envy to arise within them. Jealousy puts you in a state of mind to anticipate danger or something evil happening without any conscious reasoning. Jealousy makes you possessive, suspicious, and paranoid.

When I think of the word anger, words such as mad, rage, temper, hostility, fury, and wrath come to mind. The word anger means an intense emotional state induced by displeasure. When a person is angry, it is their actions or behaviors that conveys the condition of their emotional state. Anger is a common term that labels or titles the actions or behaviors motivated by anger. But anger itself conveys nothing about intensity or manifestation of the emotional state.

When a person is fueled with rage and loses all emotional self-control and commits acts of violence. We say the person was angry, so they lost emotional self-control. Anger is a common term that labels their actions or behaviors of rage. But the rage is motivated by the person's anger due to their displeasure about the issue that lead to the violence. When a person is fueled with fury their destructive rage can verge on madness because they believe everyone is betraying them. We say the person was angry because they believed everyone was betraying them, so they became furious. Again, the fury was motivated by the person's anger due to their displeasure about the issue. When a person is fueled with wrath they have a desire or intent to seek revenge or punish someone they feel has caused them bodily harm. We say because of their anger they felt it necessary to seek revenge, so they punched the person. It is the anger that motivates the person's actions or behavior due to their displeasure about the issue.

When I think of the word envy, words such as hate, jealousy, malice, resentment, and grudge come to mind. The word envy means resentful desire for another's possessions or advantages. When you envy someone or the things they have you are simply jealous of them. You envy them because you want to emulate or imitate who they are. You wish you were them. This is because you lack the quality of mind or temperament that enables you to stand firm in your beliefs and follow your inner wisdom to create for yourself the life you desire.

Being envious of someone can lead to malicious behavior because you develop an unexplainable desire to see that person suffer for no apparent reason. You become spiteful of the person and your feelings of resentment begin to show with expressions of harassment, such as insults and rumors.

You have a deep passion and relentlessness to see them fail that is motiveless. You hold a grudge toward the person harboring feelings of ill will and resentment and you do not have an answer as to why.

When you have emotions of jealousy, anger, and envy you are headed down a path of destruction. Jealousy, anger, and envy breathes life into each other's existence. When you are jealous of someone you are resentful and envious of that person. When you envy someone, you are jealous of them and have resentment toward them. This is a multiple dosage of jealousy, envy, and resentment toward that person. It is your jealousy, envy, and resentment toward that person that causes you to develop anger toward that person.

Now as we discussed earlier, anger is the common term that labels or titles a person's actions or behavior due to their displeasure. This displeasure includes jealousy, envy, resentment, or any other negative emotional feelings. So, it is fair to say that because of a person's jealousy or envy they develop anger that motivates harmful emotional actions and behaviors that can lead to destructive violence such as rage, fury, wrath, malignity, malice, malevolence, spite, harassment, etc., etc. This is why I say negative emotions breathes life into other negative emotions and they love all the company they can get.

One of my favorite stories in the Bible that illustrates the dangerous capabilities of these negative emotions is the story of Cain and Abel. To tell you a little about these two, Cain was the first human child born. He was the first to follow in his father's profession of farming. But he was also the first murderer. Abel was the second human child born. He was the first of his profession of a shepherd. He was also the first person to be murdered, and he was murdered by his brother Cain. Let's examine the story of Cain and Abel.

"Adam made love to his wife Eve, and she became pregnant and gave birth to Cain. She said, "With the help of the LORD I have brought forward a man." Later she gave birth to his brother Abel. Now Abel kept flocks, and Cain worked the soil. In the course of time Cain brought some of the fruits of the soil as an offering to the LORD. And Abel also brought an offering-fat portions from some of the first born of his flock. The LORD looked with favor on Abel and his offering, but on Cain and his offering he did not look with favor. So, Cain was angry, and his face was downcast.

Then the LORD said to Cain "Why are you angry? Why is your face downcast? If you do what is right, will you not be accepted? But if you do not do what is right, sin is crouching at your door, it desires to have you, but you must rule over it." Now Cain said to his brother Abel, "Lets go out to the field." While they were in the field, Cain attacked his brother Abel and killed him." -Genesis 4:1-8

Because Cain's offering had been rejected by God and Abel's offering was accepted by God, Cain became jealous, angry, and envious of his brother Abel. Cain's attitude and emotions were wrong from the start, but Cain also had a choice. He could correct his attitude about his offering or he could allow jealousy, anger, and envy to rule the throne of his soul and take his negative emotions out on his brother. Cain chose to kill his brother. We must understand that we have a choice to maintain a positive attitude and rid our soul of jealousy, anger, and envy. We may not go to the extent of murder, but these negative emotions of jealousy, anger, and envy are the motivating factors toward our dysfunctional behavior. We must begin to clear our mind, soul, and spirit of these negative emotions before they lead to actions that we may later regret.

Jealousy, anger, and envy are negative emotions that are created from within. They are negative feelings that represent fear, unfaithfulness, and displeasure. They produce a negative emotional state that can bring about violent and destructible behavior. Whenever you feel these negative emotions, it is an inner expression that something is wrong within, and you need to change these emotions right away. The way you are feeling is always an indication of what you are thinking or what is on your mind, your thoughts. If you are feeling bad you are having bad or unpleasant thoughts in your mind. When you are feeling good you are having good or pleasant thoughts.

You cannot feel bad and have good thoughts. Our mind does not work that way. Your thoughts will always tell you how you are feeling, and your feelings will always represent your thoughts. That is why it is important for you to always feel good. You need to always keep a positive emotional state. When you let emotions of jealousy, anger, and envy control your life, you do not utilize the creative power of your subconscious mind to create your desires. You are utilizing it to produce more conditions, more circumstances, and more surroundings for you to feel jealousy, anger, and envy.

When these emotions are the foundation of your attitude, you will continue to create more undesirable consequences in your life. When you have these adverse feelings, you are allowing others, conditions, circumstance, and surroundings to control your emotions. Not having control of your emotions and controlling negative thoughts, is detrimental to the creation of your ideas and desires. You have to feel good and trust the ideas and desires, you are creating through your subconscious mind. The great thing about all of this is that you can begin right now to change your emotional state and your thoughts.

You can begin to replace jealousy with love and build the belief, courage, and confidence you need within to create your ideas and desires. You can begin to replace anger with calmness, quietness, and peace. Begin to free yourself from the displeasures of emotional distress and agitation of an undesirable life, so that you can fully benefit from the effects of prayer and meditation. You can begin to replace envy with happiness. You can start having pleasurable satisfaction in the accomplishments and success of others. Realizing that you no longer live from a life of lack, and that there is plenty to go around. Getting rid of the belief and thoughts of "It should have been me."

We must learn to rejoice in happiness concerning the positive success and achievements of others. These positive emotions create vibrant waves of success, happiness, and joy into our lives. Reinforcing the beliefs of our ideas and desires onto our subconscious mind. We must stop living our lives like crabs in a bucket pulling each other down, not wanting to see the success of others, because we lack the belief, faith, ideas, and desires to create the life we want for ourselves. We can no longer allow jealousy, anger, and envy to rule the throne of our soul and be the dictators of our life.

Let's restore our thoughts and emotions to work in favor of our desires by controlling our thoughts and maintaining a positive emotional state. Happiness, success, joy, love, wealth, and prosperity all comes from within. So, let's stop "trying "to be happy and change our attitude by "doing" the things that are necessary to create the happiness we desire, because "trying is not doing." Before we can change what is on the outside, we first must change what is on the inside. We start by changing our habitual thoughts, maintain a positive emotional state, believing in ourselves, and the creative power of our subconscious mind.

FEAR AND DOUBT

THE FIRST DUTY OF MAN IS TO CONQUER FEAR; HE MUST GET RID OF IT, HE CANNOT ACT TILL THEN.

-THOMAS CARLYLE

FEAR AND DOUBT

When discussing the words fear and doubt, let's examine what they mean. The word fear means to be afraid of or apprehensive. It is an unpleasant often strong emotion caused by anticipation or awareness of danger. It implies anxiety and usually loss of courage. The word doubt means to lack confidence in, to be uncertain. It is uncertainty of belief or opinion that often interferes with decision making; a deliberate suspension of judgement. The word fear and doubt are highly associated with one another. Fear and doubt causes a destructive energy or power to be exerted over the mind and soul of unbelief or negative belief. Positive beliefs build you up, but fear and doubt tear you down.

Fear and doubt should be eliminated from your existence for the necessary growth and development of your thinking. When you have thoughts and emotions of fear and doubt you will hinder yourself from the accomplishments of your creative thoughts, ideas, and desires. With fear and doubt in the driver seat of your thoughts and emotions, they will always lead you to failure. They will eliminate any positive thoughts you may have and drain you of any positive emotional power you may have. They will not allow you to be productive in utilizing the creative power of your subconscious mind. Fear and doubt, discourages you and makes you close minded to the direction of knowledge for the conquering of your desires.

Until you conquer fear and doubt you will never conquer failure or success. Because failure of success is the fruit that is brought forth by fear and doubt, that will cause your ideas and desires to fall prematurely to the ground, because they have not had the proper time to mature. When you allow fear and doubt to enter your thoughts and emotions, they eventually find a resting place in your mind, heart, and soul. They grow and strengthen within you. You become accustom to them and challenge every opportunity of productiveness with negativity. You discourage yourself away from your creative thoughts and ideas, because you lack the self-confidence to take advantage of the favorable circumstances that are presented to you. You will never accomplish anything as long as fear and doubt controls your thoughts and emotions.

That is why every book of faith teaches the significance of ridding your thoughts and emotions of fear and doubt. They teach us the importance of our belief and faith in our Divine Source to provide for us whatever it is our heart desires. Now I believe a person's beliefs and their faith can be two different things. I believe a person's faith can be based more upon their theological belief. By faith you receive Jesus as the only one that can save you from sin, so you live out your faith by obeying his commands. It is a person's opinion or intellectual point of view. For me a person's beliefs are based or developed from their mind, heart, and soul. So, when I speak of belief and having faith, I am referring to what is in a person's heart and what they think about themselves. *"For as he thinks in his heart so is he." -Proverbs 23:7*

I believe what is in a person's mind, heart, and soul reveals who they are. It is the beliefs, that governs a person's thoughts and emotions that is exposed in their life. It is the beliefs of a person, about their creative thoughts and ideas that sends their conscious mind into action to impress their true desires onto their subconscious mind. Because your beliefs are the emotional convictions of your soul. It is through your beliefs and faith in God, that you rid your thoughts and emotions of any fear and doubt. Belief is a state of habit of mind in which trust or confidence is placed. It is conviction of the truth of some statement or the reality of some being or phenomenon.

Belief in oneself is the basic principle of all accomplishments. It demolishes any existence of fear and doubt. It is impossible for a person with positive beliefs of "I can", "I will", and "I am able" to believe in fear and doubt. Negative beliefs of fear and doubt cannot survive in the soul where beliefs of courage, mettle, and tenacity lives. A person's beliefs are proven through their actions. It is your belief in the creative power of your subconscious mind that you are able to utilize the workings of the creative process for the benefit of your life. That is why when you have negative thoughts, with negative emotions. And deep down in your soul there is the negative convictions of belief about your abilities to overcome your negative conditions, circumstances, and surroundings your subconscious mind creates more of this negativity. Because your thoughts, emotions, and beliefs are in harmonious agreement with each other. Your negative thoughts, your negative emotions, confirmed by your negative beliefs.

That is why, it is very important to rid fear and doubt out of your existence and replace them with positive beliefs of resolution, fortitude, perseverance, and determination. There are only two types of beliefs you can have. The good beliefs that represent the positive or bad beliefs that represent the negative or unbelief. It is the good or bad beliefs in your mind, heart, and soul that creates your life. If you believe you can do it, your will do it. If you believe you cannot do it, you will not do it.

It is what you believe, the beliefs about yourself that is the reflection of your life. Begin to eliminate the negative beliefs of fear and doubt and replace them with positive beliefs. You will begin to accomplish all of your heart's desires. You will start to regain the necessary confidence to believe in yourself, your thoughts, your ideas, and your dreams. You will begin to flip the switch of the creative power of your subconscious mind.

THE POWER OF FORGIVENESS

LET YOUR PAST BE A LEARNING EXPERIENCE AND NOT A CONFIRMING EXPERIENCE.

-FREDRICK MOORE

THE POWER OF FORGIVENESS

When I think about the word forgiveness, words such as excuse, pardon, and the phrase "forgive and forget" comes to mind. The word forgive means to give up resent of or claim to requital for; To cease to feel resentment against; to grant forgiveness. Forgiveness is a deed that we should exercise throughout our daily lives. The Bible states *"Do not judge, and you will not be judge. Do not condemn, and you will not be condemned. Forgive and you will be forgiven." Luke 6:37* For most of us this is easier said than done.

I mean let's be honest, it is hard to forgive someone who has wronged you, misused your trust, and has caused nothing but conflict and chaos in your life. It is hard to forget with all the habitual thoughts of "who do she think she is to do me like this," "I believed everything he said to me and he played me," " This is the last time I trust someone," "I am a fool for letting this happen," "If I was not so weak, people would not take advantage of me," "I am so dumb," "I am so stupid,"….the thoughts goes on and on. What we must understand is, without forgiveness these thoughts will continue to haunt us for our entire lives. These negative thoughts and emotions of bitterness, self-doubt, self-pity, and anger will continue to hold us back from accomplishing our desires and ideas through the creative power of our subconscious mind.

The real power of overcoming any disappointment, resentment, hate, and wrong doings caused by ourselves and others, is to forgive and move on. When we honestly forgive from our soul, it restores the power back into our lives that we have been wasting on grudges, resentment, self-pity, hate, bitterness, etc. Forgiveness is acceptance within your spirit to forgive, learn from, and move on no matter what the misdeed is. When you are unable to forgive you allow yourself, the person, and the misdeed to hold you back from achieving your desires. Your power is geared toward others, the event, and the negative emotions that being unforgiving possess. Disagreements and betrayals will always occur but learning to forgive is rising above it.

Being forgiving does not make you a weak person, in fact it strengthens you and builds character. It allows you to put all misdeeds behind you, so that you can remain focused on your desires. Being forgiving allows you to be open-minded about any situation. Ensuring that you never play the victim. Because when you victimize yourself you open the doors to vindicate negative emotions that can lead to retaliation and revenge. We must get rid of our eye for an eye attitude and rise above any conflicts or betrayal that we may experience.

We must also learn to forgive ourselves and let go of the burdens within. We must release the guilt, shame, anger, and self-doubt of our past experiences and failures. Forgiveness replaces negative emotions with positive emotions within your spirit and soul. God's love begins to fill your spirit and soul with emotions of peace, joy, and happiness. Having the power to forgive is having the power to love. So, begin to love yourself and others with the power of forgiveness. Begin to build confidence, worthiness, and deservedness to be what you desire to be. You will begin to create the positive spirit that is required to utilize the creative power of your subconscious mind.

Forgiveness creates positive emotions, because you start to release the negative emotions of doubt, regret, fear, self-pity, revenge, and anger. With forgiveness you begin to trust again, you learn from the forgiving situation, and you do not allow it to drain power away from you. You start to view each situation as a learning experience, acknowledging that one situation has nothing to do with the other. You build confidence in the creative power of your subconscious mind. Developing the beliefs needed to reinforce your ideas, desire, and mental images of love, success, wealth, prosperity, and abundance. Forgiveness removes the negative barriers of your emotions that is stopping you from accomplishing your desires due to past experiences. It allows you to relinquish the negative emotions of resentment, guilt, abandonment, distrust, fear, etc., enabling you to move into harmony and agreement with the positive ideas and mental images that are being impressed onto your subconscious mind.

Refusing to forgive and holding onto grudges of any kind leads to emotional congestion in your spirit and soul, which in return will only produce more negative conditions, circumstances, and surroundings. When you forgive, you are in control of your emotions. Controlled emotions allow you to control your thoughts, putting you in the driver seat of the creative power of your subconscious mind. Forgive, learn from the experience, and move on. Some of us just will not accept the misdeeds, broken heartedness, conflicts, and broken trust as a learning experience and move on from it. We dwell on the hurt, anger, deceit, and mistrust. The negative emotions that continue to block the creative ideas of our desires.

We get so focused on revenge that it becomes the center of attraction in our lives. We create ways and ideas to be vengeful, instead of creating ideas to be successful. "So, what they did not apologize," it is better not to receive an apology, then to get one that is not sincere and honest. We must learn to control the things in our lives that we can control and learn to let the rest go. We will never be able to control the actions of others and you should not want to be able to control the actions of others. You are responsible for your actions, and your actions alone. You are the one responsible for letting go of the anger, hate, self-pity, and pain that you are holding on to because you choose to be unforgiving.

    Forgiveness shows maturity and growth from within. It brings peace to your soul and the souls of others. You free yourself and others from the shackles of negative emotions. You direct your energy and your power toward the creation of positive ideas to your subconscious mind. God has blessed us with the gifts of His grace and mercy, and our ability to forgive is a reproduction of those gifts He has given to us. Restore the power you have within you, that you have been allowing others to drain from you, utilize your power to forgive.

DEFINING YOUR RELATIONSHIPS

ANY MAN MAY EASILY DO HARM, BUT NOT EVERY MAN CAN DO GOOD TO ANOTHER.

-PLATO

DEFINING YOUR RELATIONSHIPS

When I think of the word relationship, words such as relative, spouse, friend, and lover come to mind. The word relationship means the state of being related or interrelated: a romantic or passionate attachment. When I speak about defining your relationships, I am referring to you evaluating your past, current, and future relationships. Now, I for one believe in leaving the past in the past. But I like to evaluate my past relationships to examine any patterns I might have, that has affected my current relationships, and to prevent them from effecting my future relationships.

If you are currently in an unhealthy relationship I will say this, you deserve better, move on. Our relationships have a major effect on us mentally and emotionally. They also effect how we respond to others as well. For me an unhealthy relationship is a relationship that produces negative emotions, that influences your behavior in a negative manner. You are in an unhealthy relationship if it continually leaves you feeling emotionally drained, jealous, worthless, undeserving, guilty, angry, upset, unmotivated, envious, scared, controlled, not valued, controlling, and any other negative emotion you can think of.

If you impose your will on someone and instill these negative emotions upon someone, influencing their thoughts in a negative manner, you are in an unhealthy relationship. You are causing damage to another person mentally and emotionally. You need to do some serious soul searching within yourself and get to the core of your issues. Relationships should be inspiring and meaningful. They should be full of love, promote growth, and support. Relationships should be encouraging and motivating.

Here is the thing, if you are allowing someone to influence or control your emotions and thoughts negatively, you are going to continue to be in this cycle until you make the conscious decision to leave or move on. This dysfunctional pattern of thoughts did not just occur. This is a reflection of past relationships that you need to resolve and bring closure to or forgive your past and move on. It is very necessary that you deal with this issue. You will not be able to move forward in life until you do so. Negative emotions, plus negative thoughts, plus negative beliefs, equal negative conditions, circumstances, and surroundings. If you continue to allow someone to treat you in this manner, nothing will ever change.

You are not responsible for the way someone think or act. You are not responsible for their thoughts and emotions. Do not ever accept or believe anyone telling you that you are the reason they act the way they do. They are justifying their behavior and blaming you. If this is what is being said to you, tell them you are going to solve that problem for them and leave. You and only you have the power to control your thoughts and emotions.

No one can make you happy but yourself. Happiness is developed from within. You must be happy with yourself, before you can ever be happy with someone else. The reason I say no one can make you happy, because if it is people that makes us happy, then happiness is just a temporary emotion that is depended upon that person being in our lives. That is not true.

Real happiness starts from within. It starts with you being comfortable with yourself, feeling good about yourself, accepting who you are, and being confident with it. Happiness inspires and is contagious. When you are happy to see someone, it is because the vibrant waves of joy and happiness flows from within the both of you, causing a sense of excitement for the other person. Their presence enhances what is already inside of you. Your happiness is already there.

Bringing closure and forgiveness to past relationships will allow your current and future relationship to be constructive and positive. When you begin to promote positive thoughts, positive emotions, and positive beliefs within your relationships, your relationships will start to grow and become everything that you want them to be. You will begin to attract people in your life to be supportive, encouraging, and inspirational. Your subconscious mind will start to attract to you, positive, happy, joyous people that are capable of helping you accomplish your thoughts, ideas, and desires.

We must be careful of the people we allow in our lives. We cannot afford to let the negative thoughts, emotions, and beliefs of others to influence our lives. Our relationships should be based on love, faith, hope, joy, and happiness. You begin to change your life by changing your thoughts, emotions, and beliefs. Our relationships must begin to represent the ideal of our positive thoughts, emotions, and beliefs.

If you are in an unhealthy relationship, I urge you to reevaluate that relationship. If it is with a parent or relative, get an understanding and bring some closure to your issues. If it is with a friend or a lover, get some understanding and get the issues resolved. If you are unable to reach closure or resolve your issues, I suggest that you put that situation behind you and move on.

Whether you are being oppressed or being the oppressor in a relationship, both of you have some unresolved issues. Both of you need to get to the core of your issues. Seeking professional help will assist you in exploring why you allow people to treat you in such a negative way, or why you treat people in such a negative way. Most of us get defensive or embarrassed when the talk of seeking professional help is discussed with us. Well I am here to tell you, I have gotten it, I know of several people that has gotten it, and I highly recommend it.

We go to a professional doctor when we are physically sick. Well we need to see a professional doctor, also when we are mentally and emotionally sick. Dealing with issues that helps you get to the core of your problems that are affecting you mentally and emotionally, will have a positive effect on your thoughts and emotions. You will begin to have some understanding as to why you allow others to manipulate and treat you in a negative way. You will also begin to have some understanding, as to why you find it necessary to manipulate and treat people in such a negative way. Getting to the core of these issues could begin to change your entire perception of life. It could help you begin to establish positive thoughts and positive emotions. By exploring answers as to why you accept and do the things you do, could change your life forever.

HAVING SELF-CONFIDENCE

WE BUT HALF EXPRESS OURSELVES, AND ARE ASHAMED OF THAT DIVINE IDEA WHICH EACH OF US REPRESENT. IT MAY BE SAFELY TRUSTED AS PROPORTIONATE AND OF GOOD ISSUE, SO IT BE FAITHFULL IMPARTED, BUT GOD WILL NOT HAVE HIS WORK MADE MANIFEST BY COWARDS.

-RALPH WALDO EMERSON

HAVING SELF-CONFIDENCE

Having self-confidence is absolutely necessary while working towards accomplishing your ideas and desires. The meaning of self-confidence is having confidence in oneself and in one's powers and abilities. Believing in yourself and the creative power of your subconscious mind is a fundamental principle of the creative process in utilizing your subconscious mind. Self-confidence is one of those qualities that flows from within. But not all of us believe in ourselves and the capabilities we have. Most of us lost the confidence within ourselves a long time ago.

It could be due to the conditions and the environment we grew up in, constantly looking at the poverty and crime all around us. Not realizing that there is more to life than what we see. Thinking and believing that these drug infested neighborhoods is all there is to life. It's been implanted in our mind and soul that due to our conditions, circumstances, and surroundings we will never be anyone great and we will never do anything great with our lives. We digest in our mind and soul the thoughts and beliefs that our families did not amount to anything great, so neither will we. We look at generation after generation of drug addicts, drug dealers, prostitution, and poverty. We suffer from a lack of education, opportunities, and positive influences in our lives.

So, we just go on day by day asking ourselves "why doesn't anyone care about us," or why doesn't someone help us." We play the victim and reinforce our beliefs that we never had a chance, because of who we are and the conditions, circumstances, and surroundings we grew up in. We live our lives yearning and wishing for a better life, but self-doubt and distrust has flooded our minds and souls. We have become accustomed to a life of lack, so we start to believe that there is not enough to go around for everyone. We start to become jealous and envious of one another becoming angry about the success of others. We develop what I call the crabs in a bucket syndrome, because as soon as we see a glimpse of ambition, hope, or confidence in the eyes of someone we know or that is close to us, we tear them down with our words of discouragement. Trying to pull them back into the same negative mind state that we are in.

It is like the fear of seeing them achieve their desires takes over our spirit and we go into survival mode as if our life is in danger. Doing everything we can to pull them down. Feelings of hopelessness fills our spirit with negative emotions asking ourselves "why not me," or "what did they do to deserve the success that is happening to them." We continue to throw a pity party within our self for our self, creating more negative conditions, circumstances, and surroundings in our lives. But the saddest part of all about this dysfunctional behavior, is that we pass these negative thoughts, emotions, and beliefs onto our children and they will pass them onto their children. Continuing to create generational curses and living a life that is undesirable, due to our lack of self-confidence and our ignorance of the creative power of our subconscious mind.

We must acknowledge the fact that our subconscious mind does not care about our past. We must leave our past behind us. We must accept the fact that we cannot change anything that has happened in our past, "so what I grew up poor," "so what my business failed," "so what I disappointed some people." We must accept and understand that failure is a part of life. Everything and anything you have failed at should be a learning experience for you. You now know what to do and what not to do. You now know what works for you and what do not work for you.

The creative power of your subconscious mind will direct you and create the conditions, circumstances, and surroundings of your desires. Most of us try and do things without seeking the guidance from within. We impose our own will on a situation instead of seeking the guidance of the Will of God. Our subconscious mind is One with God. He is the only Source, the only Power that provides guidance, provides direction, and provides the creative power of our subconscious mind. Our self-confidence of this power from within strengthens our belief in our thoughts, desires, ideas, and the mental images we hold in our mind about ourselves and our abilities.

Let's take a bird for example, a bird is born with the ability to fly. They watch their mother fly to and from the nest to bring them food. Not realizing they too have the ability to fly. When it becomes time for them to learn how to fly, she forces them out of the nest to use the abilities they were born with. Some of the birds learn or grasp the idea of flying quicker than the others. But it is their self-confidence that is strengthen in each of these birds about themselves and their God given abilities, every time they make progress in properly using their abilities. After a while flying becomes natural for them.

These same principles apply to the creative power of your subconscious mind. You are born with the ability to create your ideas and desires by utilizing the power of your subconscious mind. The more you use it the more confident you become. After a while using this power will become natural for you. You do not need anything extra or special for it to work. You do not need no one to do anything special for you to make it work. Besides, they cannot make it work for you anyway. You are the only person that can utilize the creative power of your subconscious mind. Your self-confidence and belief in your abilities is something that comes from within. You must believe in yourself and have faith in your creative abilities that you have been blessed with from God or whatever Higher Power Name you may call Him.

We cannot continue to be afraid to follow our dreams, because we are worried about what other people may think or say. We must have self-confidence in our own thoughts and ideas even when others may disagree. But I am really dumbfounded by the fact that we value the ideas of others and tradition more than our own thoughts, ideas, and intuitions. We are so quick and ready to run in the direction and beat of everyone else's drum, but not to the vibrant beat of our own heart desires. It is like we are afraid to think for ourselves, because we do not believe in ourselves, always wanting the approval of others.

Ralph Waldo Emerson explained it best, when he stated, "To believe your own thoughts, to believe that what is true for you in your private heart is true for all men- that is genius." We need to trust ourselves and believe in the creative power of our subconscious mind. Every one of you that is reading this book is a unique individual. We were put here to enjoy the life, love, and beauty this world has to offer. But we will not fulfill that enjoyment being cowards, because we are afraid to believe in ourselves and do that thing our Divine Source is leading us to do.

We must accept the fact that we are unique, and tradition may have worked for others, but it is just not for us. No one can tell you how you feel or what you should be thinking. They are not God! We must learn to listen to that burning intuition of our soul, so that the light God is shining in us, is allowed to shine through us for the world to see. We cannot afford to continue letting society and tradition dictate our lives. We are each put here to express our own ideas. We must rid ourselves of the humiliated feelings of guilt, shame, disgrace, and unacceptability, by fully expressing ourselves through the marvelous ideas that represent us. We must be prepared to say no to others and traditions if they do not exist within our truth.

When I think about having self-confidence and doing the thing that works for you even if it means stepping out of the box of tradition and doing what feels right to you. I think about the story of David and Goliath. David started out as a shepherd, he tended to his father's sheep. But by the time David's life story ended his occupations would read Shepherd, Musician, Poet, Soldier, and King. Yes, this young man took himself from tending to his father's sheep unto becoming the Greatest King of Israel. I invite you to read 1Samuel, it is an intriguing and inspiring story of the Bible to me.

But the verses I want to discuss is *1Samuel 17:38-40* *"Then Saul dressed David in his own tunic. He put a coat of armor on him and a bronze helmet on his head. David fastened on his sword over the tunic and tried walking around, because he was not used to them. "I cannot go in these" he said to Saul, "because I am not used to them." So he took them off. Then he took his staff in his hand, chose five smooth stones from the stream, put them in the pouch of his shepherd's bag, and with his sling in his hand approached the Philistine."* David defeated Goliath, but he had to go into battle the way he felt comfortable in going.

God had prepared David during the course of his life as a shepherd for this very moment. David had battled and killed wild animals that may have tried to carry off one of his sheep, so he was use to going into battle the way that most of us would probably view as being over matched. But as for David, he believed with absolute certainty that God was on his side and the same God that protected him in his battles as a shepherd would protect him in his battle as a soldier. So instead of conforming to the tradition of wearing the heavy armor gear that all soldiers were accustomed to wearing, David said to Saul "I cannot go in these," "because I am not used to them." David had to do what was natural in his heart. He had the self-confidence within and faith in God. He did not care what Saul, or the other soldiers may have thought. He believed that God had prepared him and would protect him in his battle. He was not comfortable in the heavy armor, he knew it was not for him, so he was not going to pretend and conform to tradition, so he took it off.

    We must develop the self-confidence, the self-esteem, and the courage of David to be able to tell whoever it may concern, I must be myself. I need to do my thing, my way. Because your way, I am not use to and I do not feel comfortable doing things your way. We must start taking off the opinions of others, the seeking approval of others, the tradition of others, and begin to trust our own way of thinking, feeling, and doing. God has equipped each of us with the tools we need within, to live a fulfilled life of love, peace, wealth, happiness, and abundance. So, begin to believe in yourself, your abilities, and the creative power of your subconscious mind and create the life you desire to have for yourself.

CLEARING YOUR LINES OF COMMUNICATION

YOU HAVE TO BELIEVE IN YOURSELF.

-SUN TZU

CLEARING YOUR LINES OF COMMUNICATION

Before I start on this section about clearing your lines of communication let's be clear on one thing. You have the ability to create, but God is the Creator. So, let's not get anything I say misunderstood. He has given us the power to create, within the world that He has created. So, that the Spirit may enjoy and experience Life, Love, and Beauty through us. You and only you have the capabilities to create your ideas and desires. You do not need anyone to communicate with God for you. You were born with everything you need to make a connection on your own. You have access to Him, 24 hours a day, 7 days a week, because it is within you where He dwells.

We access Him by communicating and making a connection through our subconscious mind. The reason most of us cannot make the connection we want, is because we are sending the wrong messages through our lines of communication. There is so much confusion, chaos, and lawlessness going on in our thoughts, emotions, and beliefs, that our lines of communication are muddled. The wrong messages are being sent and due to our ignorance, we go through our daily lives with our thoughts, emotions, and beliefs on auto pilot or should I say auto suggestion.

We let our negative conditions, circumstances, and surroundings dictate our suggestive thoughts. Our thoughts and emotions are focused on our negative conditions, circumstances, and surroundings, being supported by our negative beliefs toward our negative conditions, circumstances, and surroundings. Validating to our subconscious mind that these are our desires. Therefore, our subconscious mind is only responding to what we are telling it. So, our subconscious mind starts creating more of the negative conditions, circumstances, and surroundings that we do not want.

But because we are unaware of this, the auto pilot or auto suggestion stays on and we continue to live our lives in this vicious cycle. Now I am not saying or suggesting that this is what anyone wants, but when we focus our thoughts and emotions along with the belief of not being able, not accomplishing, or not wanting, this is what we create. A life of undesirable conditions, circumstances, and surroundings, because these are the thoughts and ideas that our habitual thinking is focused on. A life of not being able, not accomplishing, and not wanting. By comprehending this, you begin to understand how you have created a life that is undesirable to you. But the good news is, now that you understand your ability to create, you can change these things around and start to create the life that you desire, by flipping the switch of the creative power of your subconscious mind.

You begin by taking your thoughts, your emotions, and your beliefs off of auto pilot or auto suggestion, and you begin to control your thoughts and emotions to clear the lines of communication between you and God. By controlling your thoughts and emotions you can clearly and assertively impress upon your subconscious mind what it is that you really want, what it is that you truly desire. Removing the confusion, chaos, and lawlessness that is distorting your lines of communication through your subconscious mind. By controlling your emotions, you begin to produce emotions that is a representation of your thoughts, bringing your thoughts, ideas, beliefs, and emotions into a positive harmonious agreement with each other. Creating the positive conditions, circumstances, and surroundings your heart desires. When you control your emotions, you are aware of how you feel and the thoughts that are running through your mind, your habitual thoughts.

Controlled positive thoughts, controlled positive emotions, and belief in yourself leads to the enlightenment of the creative power of your subconscious mind. It guides you to the creation, manifestation, and materialization of your ideas, mental images, and desires. This is how the law of attraction works and it will never fail you, because it has never failed anyone. All the energy we put into pondering over what we do not want, direct that energy towards what it is that you really want. Remain focused on it until it consumes every thought of your existence. Learn these principles to utilize your ability to create, it should become a priority in your life, if changing your life is a priority.

Prayer and meditation are ways to clear your mind and spirit of confusion, chaos, and lawlessness. Allowing you to free your thoughts and emotions, and move them into a positive state of calmness, quietness, and stillness. This allows you to communicate assertively with God through your subconscious mind. Expressing a clear and harmonious thought, idea, and mental image that is of one accord with your emotions and beliefs.

So, when I stated earlier that your subconscious mind is amenable to suggestion, this is exactly what I am talking about. The word suggestion means the process by which a physical or mental state is influenced by a thought or idea: the process by which one thought leads to another especially through association of ideas. Therefore, it is through our beliefs, our convictions, our faith, and the acceptance that a suggestion, thought, idea, or mental image is already true. Our conscious mind impresses these, suggestions thoughts, ideas, or mental images onto our subconscious mind awakening a desire to be created, manifested, and materialized.

    In knowing this it eliminates your ignorance, making you aware of the importance of clearing your lines of communication. You can now remove your thoughts, emotions, and beliefs off of auto pilot or auto suggestion by flipping the switch of the creative power of your subconscious mind. You can now sit in the driver seat of your mind and control the thoughts, ideas, and mental images that has been dictating your life. You can now sit in the driver seat of your emotions, not letting your conditions, circumstances, and surroundings dictate how you feel. This will enable you to have your positive beliefs, thoughts, ideas, mental images, emotions, and desires all on one accord.

    Allowing you to utilize your abilities, and create a life that is full of joy, love, and beauty. This permits you to enjoy a life full of wealth, health, prosperity, and abundance. This puts you in the driver seat to use your creative abilities, and clearly communicate whatever it is that you truly desire. *"Ask and it will be given to you; seek and you will find; knock and the door will be opened to you. For everyone who ask receives; the one who seeks finds; and the one who knocks, the door will be opened." Matthew 7:7-8*

LET ME SAY THIS

" No good tree bears bad fruit nor does a bad tree bear good fruit. Each tree is recognized by its own fruit." Luke 6:43-44, When I look at this Bible verse I understand that the tree is the producer of the fruit. So, the tree represents my thoughts, my habitual thinking, and the fruit represent the results in life that I receive from these thoughts. So, it is stated in the Bible clear as day that no good thought produces bad results and no bad thought produces good results. The fruit of life is in our thinking. Our life is the result of the habitual thoughts we are thinking.

For us to begin to create the generational blessings of love, wealth, joy, abundance, and prosperity, we must first believe we are deserving to be those things. We must strengthen our confidence and belief that we are capable of being loved, being wealthy, being joyous, being abundant, and being prosperous by changing the way we think and feel about things. Starting with ourselves, our conditions, our circumstances, our surroundings, and the things we have right now. We must flip the switch of our subconscious mind and begin to utilize its creative power. By understanding that we are united with God's Mind through our subconscious mind, we must be aware of the mental images we are placing on our subconscious mind and the condition of our emotional state. It is our thoughts that are producing the life we are living, so when we change our habitual thoughts to positive ones that produces love, wealth, joy, abundance, and prosperity, those conditions will become the products of our lives.

Keeping a positive emotional state is very important when utilizing the creative power of your subconscious mind. You must feel good about yourself, have faith, and believe that you are capable of achieving your desires. Feelings of love, joy, and happiness are developed from within, when you start to develop an intimate relationship with the Divine Source. You do this through your beliefs, faith, and acceptance of your creative power within. Understanding, who's you are, your purpose, and birthright, will help inspire, restore, and encourage your beliefs in the creative power of your subconscious mind. We must create positive thoughts that produces positive emotions of love, life, and beauty, the inherent essence of our existence.

    Start to surround yourself with positive people that encourages, uplifts, and supports your growth mentally and spiritually. Utilize the power of affirmation, visualization, prayer, and meditation to help strengthen your faith. Replacing emotions of jealousy, anger, and envy with love, peace, and happiness will help you remain in a positive emotional mind state. We must rid our mind of the crabs in a bucket syndrome and learn to celebrate the success of others. Promoting love, joy, and happiness toward others create vibrant waves of the same back into our lives.

    Positive emotions help us to develop a spirit that is pleasing, agreeable, and enjoyable to God. Positive emotions allow us to have a presence of mind and promotes peace from within ourselves. By learning to control our emotions we will not only start to exercise self-control but thought control as well. Negative emotions are unhealthy emotions that can get out of control, conduct violence, spiritual damage, mental stress, and emotional hurt to ourselves and others. *"For as churning cream produces butter, and as twisting the nose produces blood, so stirring up anger produces strife."- Proverbs 30:33,* A good tree will always bear good fruit.

Acknowledge your authority, your power, and your status in regard to your ability to create. We distort our minds, our thoughts, and our ideas when we concern ourselves with negative circumstances, actions, and incidents that is out of our control. We allow these things to dictate our lives by focusing on them, allowing them to control our emotions. We cannot continue to live our lives full of resentment, self-pity, bitterness, and hate. Allowing these attitudes of negative emotions to destroy our spirit devouring our soul.

We cannot continue to allow others to control our emotions by focusing our energy and thoughts on their misdeeds or mistrust. We must stop dwelling on our past allowing guilt, shame, and doubt to stop us from progressing, because we are habitually thinking about our missed opportunities and failures. We must exercise our power of forgiveness and apply it to our lives daily. We must learn to forgive ourselves as well as others of conflicts and betrayals, releasing the burdens we are holding within. Forgiveness removes the negative emotional barriers that is stopping us from achieving our desires. Forgiveness allows us to relinquish our negative emotions and allow us to be in harmonious union with our positive ideas and desires.

Forgiveness brings peace to our soul and the souls of others, developing growth and maturity from within. This permits us to restore our power within, strengthening our self-confidence. Having self-confidence, believing in yourself, and your abilities is very important. Self-confidence is a strength that comes from within. It is trusting yourself, your abilities, and your ideas knowing that you are One with God. It is not conforming to tradition but expressing yourself through the marvelous ideas that is a representation of your true self.

Having self-confidence is expressing and following your own thoughts and ideas, not concerning yourself with being humiliated or feeling guilty and disgraceful, because your thoughts and ideas are deemed by society as unconventional or different. Having self-confidence is having the courage to say no when society say yes, it is having the courage to say yes when society says no. It is having the courage to do what feels right to you despite whatever the opinions of others may be. Having self-confidence is having the courage of David, to take off the armor of society and not conform to any traditions that do not fit right with you. We must have the courage to be ourselves and follow our own thoughts, ideas, intuitions, and ambitions. We have been equipped with everything we need within, to live life the way we desire.

By understanding our ability to create through the creative power of our subconscious mind, clears up our lines of communication with The Power, The Source, The Creator, God. By controlling our thoughts and emotions reinforced by our beliefs, we are able to utilize our abilities and clearly communicate through the creative power of our subconscious mind. This allows us to live a life of love, success, happiness, wealth, and abundance. We have the ability to create whatever it is that our heart desires. Our subconscious mind has all the answers we need to determine the simplest way to accomplish our desires. Creating a mental image, visualization, prayer, meditation, writing and saying affirmations, and creating vision boards, backed by faith, confidence, and patients are just some of the ways that you can utilize the omnipotent power of your subconscious mind. *"Go! Let it be done just as you believe it would." - Matthew 8:13*, You are the mastermind of your thoughts.

SECTION III

BEING THANKFUL, SHOWING GRATITUDE, AND ENCOURAGING OTHERS

KIND WORDS DO NOT COST MUCH. YET THEY ACCOMPLISH MUCH.

-BLAISE PASCAL

BEING THANKFUL, SHOWING GRATITUDE, AND ENCOURAGING OTHERS

Having a positive attitude should be an established disposition in our lives. By repeatedly exercising a positive attitude it will become a habitual part of our character and temperament. Being thankful, showing gratitude, and encouraging others are extraordinary and distinctive qualities that can be attributed to maintaining a positive attitude. We can begin to implement these qualities into our everyday lives.

We can first start by being thankful for the grace and mercy that has been given to us. We should be thankful for being able to awake this morning and use our extremities. We should be thankful that we are able to read this book with our own eyes and have the ability to comprehend what we are reading with our own mind. We should be thankful for the things we have, the life we have, and the people that are in our lives. Even though we may view ourselves as having so little, thinking to ourselves we have such a terrible life, and that we would probably be better off without the people that is around us. We should still be thankful!

There are people out there that wish they could have our lives, because their lives are in a much worst condition than ours. There are people out there that cannot get up on their own. There are people out there who are not able to walk or are unable to use their extremities. There are people out there that cannot read a book and do not have the ability to comprehend anything because they are not in their right mind.

There are children out there that is homeless or have no choice but to live in a foster home, because their parents died or deserted them. Imagine what life must be like for these children. There are elderly people that are confined to a nursing home, because their children and love ones would not or could not take care of them. So, they have been left in a home with a stranger to take care of them. Some suffer from the loss of memory and have not been able to recognize their families for years. While the ones that have their memory, must accept the harsh reality of not seeing their children and love ones, because they have abandoned them and have not been to visit them in years.

We must learn to be thankful for the life we have right now. We must comprehend the fact that there are people in this world in a much worst state than we are. We must start being thankful for the things we may view as a little, until they become what we consider to be an abundance. We must start right now to have a thankful attitude and feel good about our lives. If you have a roof over your head, be thankful for it. If you received a meal today, be thankful for it. If you still have your job today, be thankful for it.

The people you wish were not in your life, be thankful for them. Because they are the ones that are motivating you to get up and change your life. They are the ones making you realize, that there must be more to life than what you have right now, more to life than the chaos and disorder you are dealing with right now. When we start being thankful for the positive things we have in our life right now. Our subconscious mind will start to create more positive conditions, circumstances, and surroundings into our life to be thankful for. We must begin to change our attitude and become thankful for the things we have today.

Showing gratitude is another quality we can begin to implement in our daily lives. While having an attitude of gratitude can be viewed as being thankful for what you have. I like to view showing gratitude as a way to show people you are thankful for them and the things they are doing for you in your life. What would it hurt and how much work would it take to give your mother, father, brother, sister, daughter, son, wife, husband, etc., a big hug and kiss right now, and tell them how much you love them? I am guessing nothing. What would it hurt and how much work would it take to give or send a thank you card to your spouse, sibling, co-worker, parents, neighbor, boss, children, a teacher, or a principal? Well, I am guessing nothing once again.

It is these sudden acts of kindness that are so meaningful to the lives of others, in just saying thank you, I love you, and I appreciate you. Leaving your spouse an affectionate note that say, "I love you, thank you for all that you do, and I appreciated you for being a special part of my life." It is these sudden acts of kindness that shows your gratitude for the deeds of others that are a part of your life. Showing gratitude is a way for you to show someone how you feel about them and the things they do for you. I am a true believer that action speaks louder than words and showing gratitude towards others says a lot.

Showing gratitude could be something as thoughtful as cutting your neighbors grass when you cut yours. Do the carpooling duties for the week or the month for your spouse. I am sure they would be thankful, and I bet your children will love it. Pop up at school and have lunch with your child or children. Get permission from the principal and give your child's teacher a 30-60-minute break and monitor the class for them. Help a co-worker out if you are finished with your work assignments or appointments early. If your spouse is a stay at home parent, hire a baby sitter and take them out to dinner letting them know how thankful you are for them. Spend some quality time with your parents, prepare a special dinner for them in their honor.

There are many things you can do to show your gratitude. I suggest you do it, it can strengthen your positive attitude, and attract these positive acts of kindness that you put out back into your life. When you show gratitude, it puts you in a position to do nice things for others. This provides a feel good positive spirit for you and the people you are showing gratitude toward. This feel good positive spirit puts your emotions in a harmonious agreement with your desires. This sends the message to your subconscious mind to create more situations for you to be able to enrich and enhance the lives of others through your kindness, allowing you to continuously show gratitude to the people involved in your life.

Encouraging others is the last of these unique qualities I would like to address. But it is just as important as the others. When you encourage others, you inspire them by uplifting their spirit and emboldening their self-confidence. When you tell someone how smart they are, how proud you are of them, or how much you believe in them, you reassure them of their abilities. Saying encouraging and promising words to someone can give them the strength they need to complete a task. Encouraging words builds hope, give support, and invigorates a person's self-esteem.

Telling a single parent mom how great of a job she is doing raising her child or children and how inspiring she is as a person to do such a difficult job. These are encouraging words that builds hope, give strength, and shows support. It lets her know that her hard work of being a single parent is recognized and appreciated. Offer her your support by letting her know that you believe in her, and if she needs anything you will help her in the best possible way that you can. This is what I mean by encouraging others.

Children are easily influenced, and words of encouragement are very important for their mental growth. Being overly excited and telling a child how amazing of a job they did when they accomplish something can boost their confidence about themselves. Letting a child know how proud you are of them, because they did their best, even though they may have lost or failed at something, gives the child the support they need and reassures them of their abilities. It teaches them that failing is not the end and that next time it may be a different outcome. Communicating to your daughter how beautiful and intelligent she is, especially during her adolescence years, helps her to develop the self-confidence and self-esteem she needs to believe in herself. Telling your son how much you believe in him and teaching him the importance of always being a stand-up man that always does the right things, helps him to develop courage, resolution, and fortitude.

You can begin to find ways to encourage anyone that is in your life. You can tell a co-worker how great of a job they are doing. Tell your children's coach how you appreciate the time they spend with the children and how positive of an influence they are. By making a habit of encouraging others, it will reinforce your positive attitude. Keeping your emotions in alignment with your desires. Being thankful, showing gratitude, and encouraging others creates positive vibrant vibes between you and the people you may meet. Attracting the necessary people in your life to help you achieve your ideas and desires. Also allowing you to do the same for others.

Always know that God loves you and we were created to be filled with peace, love, joy, and happiness. Be thankful for the life you have right now because things could be worst. Give someone a hug today and tell them how much you love and appreciate them. Be a blessing to someone with an uplifting word of encouragement. Being inspiring to others is contagious. It strengthens your positive attitude and faith, as well as the positive attitude and faith of others.

Being thankful, showing gratitude, and encouraging others cost you nothing, it is absolutely free to give and the benefits for doing so is very rewarding. Instilling these extraordinary and distinctive qualities into our children by setting the example will influence them in a positive way. We will begin to teach our children to give love, appreciation, and inspiration to others. Creating the generational blessings our family deserve. *"Give and it will be given to you. A good measure, pressed down, shaken together and running over, will be poured into your lap. For with the measure you use it will be measured to you."* - Luke 6:38

YOU HAVE POWER IN YOUR THOUGHTS

THOUGHT IS THE PARENT OF THE DEED.

-THOMAS CARLYLE

YOU HAVE POWER IN YOUR THOUGHTS

The word thought means the action or process of thinking. So, when I say you have power in your thoughts. I am saying you have power in your thinking. Everything and anything ever created started with a thought. Someone was thinking and came up with an idea, and that idea was materialized. We even think before we speak. So, the next time you ask someone why did they say, whatever it is that they said, and they reply to you "I wasn't thinking," tell them that is impossible. We think about what we say, before we say it.

This world we live in was created by a thought. In *Genesis 1:1* it states, *"In the beginning God created the heavens and the earth."* When we look at this in detail, we must understand the fact, that nothing can be created until it becomes a thought first. So, God thought about the heavens and the earth, then He created them. In *Genesis 1:3* it states, *"Then God said, "Let there be light;" and there was light."* When we look at this in detail, God thought about what light would be, then He created it, because the verse states "Then God said." Before we can say a thing, we must think about what it is that is going to be said, and before light could exist it had to be created by a thought. So, light was thought about, spoken into existence, and then created. This world was created with a thought by God. We have also been blessed with this awesome power of thought which allows us to create.

In Genesis 1:26-27 it states, "Then God said, "Lets Us make man in Our image, according to Our likeness; let them have dominion over the fish of the sea, over the birds of the air, and over the cattle, over all the earth and over every creeping thing that creeps on the earth." So God created man in His own image; in the image of God He created him; male and female He created them." Let us look at these text in detail. When Genesis 1:26 states "Then God said Let Us make man in Our image according to Our likeness" we must understand that the word image means a reproduction or imitation of form of a person or thing. The word likeness means copy. So, we are a reproduction, a copy of God.

Also, in Genesis 1:26 it states God gave man dominion over all the earth, and everything on it. Now the word dominion means supreme authority. The word supreme means highest in rank or authority. The word authority means a power to influence or command thought, opinion, or behavior. So, man is a reproduction of God, a copy of Him, and God also, gave man the highest power to influence and command thought, opinion, or behavior. I would like to explore this a little bit deeper.

The word influence means to affect or alter by indirect or intangible means; to have an effect on the conditions or development of. The word command means to order, or request to be given; to give orders. So, lets observer this once again. Man is a reproduction of God, a copy of Him. God also gave man the highest power to affect the conditions and development of all things, by making a request or giving orders, through his thoughts, opinions, and behaviors. Indirectly and intangibly affecting or altering all the earth and everything on it.

Our Creator, created us to be a reproduction of Himself. He has given us the power to affect our conditions, circumstances, and surroundings by making a request through our thoughts. It is the way we have been thinking that has created our undesirable conditions. Genesis 1:27 reconfirms that God created man as a reproduction of Himself, as a reproduction of God he created man. This includes male and female so just because the word "man" is used, it does not exclude the female person. We must recognize that there is a feminine and masculine element in every Being. It takes both male and female to create a child. *"Nevertheless, neither is man independent of woman, nor woman independent of man, in the Lord. For as woman came from man, even so man also come through woman; but all things are from God." -1Corinthians 11:11-12*

God created man and woman to be a reproduction of Himself. We were all created the same but was created to be different. When a man and a woman produce a child, that child is a reproduction of them both. Everything about that child's human body is the same as everyone else. Our arms and hands are designed to perform the same functions. Our legs and feet are designed to perform the same functions. Our organs are designed to perform the same functions. Even our brains, our minds work the same. But the one thing that functions differently is our thoughts. We all have the ability to think differently and to think for ourselves. We have our own thoughts, and that is what makes us unique.

We have all been given supreme authority over our thoughts to create ideas, that will be materialized and make a difference in this world. We were created to influence our conditions by the development of ideas through our thoughts. That is why I believe God has given us the power to create in this world He has created, so that the Spirit (that is God), can enjoy and experience life in us and through us. Whether you believe it or not, you have power in your thoughts. Those thoughts become ideas and mental images, which is then materialized when accepted as a true desire, by the creative power of your subconscious mind.

Our thoughts have silent power, they find the answers or solutions to any problems we may have. Our thoughts have the power and authority to guide and manage our ideas, mental images, and emotions. Our thoughts lead and instructs us to the shortest and simplest route to accomplish our ideas and desires. Our thoughts provide us with the mental and moral power to overcome any fear, anger, hatred, or doubt. Our thoughts have mystical powers, they solve, controls, directs, and conquers. You have complete control over your thoughts and that is an undeniable fact.

The most comprehensible and inspirational truth about that fact is, you have the power to control your own destiny. Do not allow the negative thoughts of others to influence the way you think. Do not allow your conditions, circumstances, and surroundings to influence the way you think. Do not allow your past to influence the way you think. You and only you can control your thoughts and emotions. But you have to control them, because if you do not control your thoughts and emotions, you will never control anything.

Your subconscious mind is omnificent, so utilize it. Your subconscious mind guides you, so seek it. Your subconscious mind answers, so ask or request it. You have power in your thoughts, and acknowledging where that power comes from, gives you the power to create and control your own fate. Wealth and completeness is within, all you have to do is access it. *"Commit your works to the LORD and your thoughts will be established." -Proverbs 16:3*

OUR LIMITLESS POWER OF THOUGHT

IF YOU CAN DREAM IT, YOU CAN DO IT.

-WALT DISNEY

OUR LIMITLESS POWER OF THOUGHT

To understand the limitless power of our thoughts, we must grasp the true significance of being created in the image and likeness of God. When discussing the image and likeness of God we must clearly understand that I am referring to an inner creation of image and likeness and not an outer creation of image and likeness. I am talking about the spirit and mind and not the body. God is Supreme Spirit, He is Omnipresent. He is present in all places at all times. He is the Omniscient of all. There is only One Spirit and it passes through all and is in all.

Thought is the movement and action of Spirit. It is thought that is the creational cause of all, it is the essential nature of a thing that is mentally separated from its matter. Thought is the conscious relation of Spirit to the individual and the entire world. It is our spirit that is created in the image and likeness of God's Spirit. So, if thought is the movement and action of His Spirit, then it is the movement and action of our spirit.

Therefore, if thought is the only action of the mind, then the image and likeness between us and god is also a mental likeness. Our mind is created in the image and likeness of God's Mind. It is the individual mind, the subconscious mind, connected as One with the Supreme Mind, God's Mind. It is the subconscious mind that represent the individual, that is a point of convergence for the Supreme Mind to give guidance, and to experience life through the consciousness of the individual. Our mind is a reproduction and copy of God's Mind. We have the inherent power of creation in our thoughts. Our thoughts have creative power and it is the awareness of our completeness and unity with God that allows us to create our lives with certainty.

We must realize that if our mind is created in the image and likeness of God's Mind, then our creative power is limitless as well. Our means or procedures used in attaining an end is different, but its quality and excellence is the same. There are no limits to thought. The creative power of our thoughts is limitless. Our minds are only limited by the thoughts we conceive.

The more limited our conceptions are the more limited our thoughts will be. We are unable to think and believe in things that we cannot conceive. So, if we do not or cannot see ourselves or imagine ourselves doing great things or being someone great, due to our conditions, circumstances, and surroundings. Our thought will be limited according to those things that influences us or that we think about the most. We limit ourselves by the thoughts that are in our mind.

It is the dwelling upon our past experiences and our current conditions, circumstance, and surroundings that limit our thoughts. We must begin to see beyond our past experiences and our current conditions, circumstances, and surroundings, by expanding our mental vision of success in order to start the development process of elevating our thoughts for the progression of our lives. The problem is, we are ignorant of our relations with God and lack the knowledge about the power of our thoughts. It is the gaining of this knowledge about our thoughts, and the acknowledgment of the ideal relations of our Oneness with God, that we begin to utilize our power from within. Failure to believe in ourselves and our power within is failure to believe in God, because it is within us where he dwells, and we are One. So, what is Supreme in God, is individual in man, our thoughts have the limitless power to create. We can achieve anything!

We must develop trust and begin to act and walk by faith and believe in the guidance and protection of God's Mind, which is the Source of the individual mind, the subconscious mind. What we must understand is, we are the ones impeding our progress by the negative thoughts we maintain with our negative habitual thinking. We are the ones impressing these negative thoughts onto our subconscious mind. We are allowing our negative external conditions, circumstances, and surroundings to dominate and control our thinking. Thus, putting us in a perpetuating cycle of generational curses and limitation. When we utilize our power this way we must understand that we are using our power in the wrong direction. It is this using our creative thought power in a negative direction that is causing us to have an attitude of misery and complaint.

We must change the direction of our thoughts by changing our method of thinking in the direction of the positive and use the inherent nature of our thought power as our starting point for creation. We must understand that creation is an inner process of mental power and not an outer process of conditions, circumstances, and surroundings. When our thoughts are focused on "not having this" or "I am not able to do that." We create more of the "not having" and the "I am not able." We create more conditions, circumstance, and surroundings to reinforce these negative thoughts and beliefs. *"For as he thinks in his heart so is he." -Proverbs 23:7*

By understanding how our thoughts work, helps us to understand that our life is a result of our thinking. We must comprehend that the changing of our habitual thoughts for the changing of our lives is a process. We must be honest about the fact that we did not construct our lives overnight. Our lives have been undesirable for many years because of our habitual negative thinking. For some it has been a life time of misery and complaint as the result of a life time of negative thinking. So, we must have patience and cannot expect things to just change overnight.

Think of your mind as a garden that needs to be cultivated because it has been allowed to run wild due to neglect. It is full of seeds (negative thoughts), that produce weeds and over time it has only produced more of its kind. As the gardener of your mind you must first refine and cultivate your mind, by tilling the soil of your mind in relations to its suitability for growth. You must keep your mind free from weeds by weeding out all the negative, destructive, and unproductive thoughts. You must grow the beautiful flowers and delicious fruits you desire by planting seeds of positive, constructive, and productive thoughts. Now patience is a must, you have to allow the seeds you have planted time to grow. You must continue to do your job as the gardener and water your seeds with knowledge and positive images, and make sure no weeds are taking root within your garden.

You will commence to comprehend that you have supreme authority of your thoughts. You are the controller of your conditions, circumstances, and surroundings. Your thoughts have brought you where you are today. For us to change the results of our lives, we must change the mental conditioning of our minds. We can no longer allow negative, impure thoughts to dominate our minds. Our outer world of conditions, circumstance, and surroundings will arise and shape themselves to the inner world of our positive thoughts.

We must begin to direct our focus of attention to "Being and Doing" and not on "Having." We do not attract wealth to us just because we want it. We attract wealth to us because that is what we are. Wealth is a product of the mind. When you realize that you are wealthy, you are healthy, and you are prosperous. You will begin to attract to your life the things that are necessary to fulfill your life as a representation of what you believe yourself to be.

We attract to us what we are and not so much as to what we want. I attract success because I AM successful. I attract wealth because I AM wealthy. I attract health because I AM healthy. When we start focusing our lives on Being and Doing the Having will come. We must refine and reeducate our minds to foster the growth of knowledge that is needed for the pleasurable development of our lives. We must start having habitual thoughts that builds us up and helps us to develop the self-confidence we need to change our lives.

By influencing our minds with constructive, affirmative, and optimistic thoughts. We will begin to impress positive images of thoughts onto our subconscious mind. Start believing you can, start believing you are able. The power of your thoughts will start to manifest conditions, circumstances, and surrounding to make these things happen. When we begin to understand the realization of the connection of the two minds as One, which is God's Mind united with the individual mind. We start to understand how our lives are created.

Misery, poverty, destruction, unhappiness etc., was not the ideal of our creation. This negativity is the creation of our inverted thinking. These things would not exist if we did not give belief to them, which in reality is giving life to them. The essence of our creation is Love, Life, and Beauty. These things represent the inherent qualities of our Being and are the elements of nature from which we should be evolving from. We should be enhancing and enriching each of these qualities through the Spirit that dwells in us, and it all starts with our individual thoughts.

We have each been given the freedom of individuality to choose our development, growth, and enjoyment of love, life, and beauty. This choosing starts with our individual thoughts. It is through the individual thoughts, that are impressed upon our subconscious mind that we communicate to God's Mind what our desires are for the development, growth, and enjoyment of our lives. This initiates the seeking of His guidance and direction. It is our will seeking the guidance and direction of His Will.

It is following His Will by faith that we begin to elevate the power of our thoughts for the development, growth, and enjoyment for our lives. When we full grasp the concept of being created in the image and likeness of God, and the limitless power of our thoughts. It is then that we will begin to experience and enjoy our lives the way we desire them to be. *"Finally brethren, whatever things are true, whatever things are noble, whatever things are just, whatever things are pure, whatever things are lovely, whatever things are of good report, if there is any virtue and if there is anything praiseworthy, meditate on these things."* -Philippians 4:8

THE EVOLUTION OF THOUGHT AND EMOTION

IDLENESS IS TO THE HUMAN MIND LIKE RUST TO IRON.

-EZRA CORNELL

THE EVOLUTION OF THOUGHT AND EMOTION

A person accomplishments, power, morality, failures, weaknesses, and immorality reflect their own thoughts and emotions. These thoughts and emotions are brought about by them and no one else can change or alter their thoughts and emotions but them. The evolution of their happiness or distress comes from within. When I speak of the evolution of thought, I am referring to the elevation of our thoughts from a lower level of thinking unto a higher level of thinking. For us to rise above our conditions, circumstances, and surroundings we must elevate our thoughts.

It is the elevation of our minds that will allow for true growth to take place in our lives. If we do not change our thought process or our way of thinking by lifting them to a higher level, we will remain idle and continue to get the same undesirable results from our lives. The creative power of our subconscious mind and our creative thoughts are limitless. We limit ourselves by the thoughts we choose and the negative emotions we reserve, because we allow our conditions, circumstances, and surroundings to dictate our thoughts and emotions. We must trust and utilize our creative thoughts, because our creative thoughts are devoted to our mental growth, our search for knowledge, and the intellectual achievements of our ideas and desires.

Thought is the only action of the mind and thinking of creative ideas is the exercising of the mind. Emotions are the creators of our spirit and soul, the foundation of our beliefs. We are the mastermind of our thoughts and the supreme controller of our emotions. Our thoughts and emotions work together for the creation of our lives. Positive thoughts and positive emotions is an untroubled harmonious state and conditioning of our mind and soul agreeing. It tells our conscious mind to impress the ideal that has brought about this harmonious conditioning onto our subconscious mind for its creation.

Our thoughts and emotions always work in agreement with each other. You cannot have good thoughts and feel bad. You cannot feel bad and have good thoughts. Our minds do not work that way. Your thoughts will always be a representation of how you feel, and your emotions will always represent your thoughts. As you begin to elevate your thoughts, your emotions will elevate as well.

Material possessions are not an indicator of you elevating your thoughts and emotions. You can acquire material possessions and your mind can still remain idle. Material possessions has nothing to do with you having positive thoughts or negative thoughts. You can be rich and unblessed, or you can be poor and blessed. When there is a positive harmonious union of your thoughts and emotions, it will lead to the positive changing of your conditions, circumstances, and surroundings. Therefore, making you blessed and wealthy. It is a positive unification of your inner thoughts and emotions that leads to the possession of health, success, prosperity, and happiness. The mental and emotional dysfunction of mishandling your conditions, circumstances, and surroundings will always deter you away from these possessions.

We were created to grow and prosper in every area of our lives and we do this through the elevation of our thoughts and emotions. We must strive to evolve our inner thoughts before any real change will take place outwardly. Even through our success and failures we are supposed to elevate and grow. But it is the way we handle our success and failures that displays the growth and elevation of our mind set. A person's conditions, circumstances, and surroundings does not dictate who they are or make them, but it reveals them. It shows how they handle success and how they handle failure. The development of their character.

Success and failure both are the mental grasping of a person's thoughts. A person's success can tell us how they handle themselves. If their new-found success is embraced with a positive attitude they will continue to grow. They continue to evolve because they remain honest, humble, objective, and open-minded to the creative power of their subconscious mind. Always allowing room for more natural growth and opportunity. As they continue to expand their thinking they will continuously evolve. They understand the creative process and they continue to follow the guidance of their subconscious mind that is One with God.

If their new-found success is embrace with a negative attitude they will not continue to grow. They will remain idle or even lower their way of thinking, because they begin to develop a self-centered attitude. They believe that it is them creating their success. The exertion of their will power. They become close-minded, hindering themselves from further natural growth and opportunity. They neglect the creative process and they are ignorant of the creative power of their subconscious mind, so they seek no guidance.

The same can be said for the person that handles failure poorly. They begin to lose all faith and hope within themselves. They allow a specific situation to dictate their entire life. They let fear and doubt consume their mind and soul, so they lack the confidence they need within themselves to overcome any obstacles in their life. They begin to create undesirable conditions, circumstances, and surroundings for themselves that is only a reflection of their thoughts and emotions. Hindering any progress to take place in their life.

Now the person that handles their failure as a learning experience and not a confirming experience will begin to naturally grow. They understand that failure is just a part of life. They realize that it is not how hard you fall, but whether you get back up or not. Their positive attitude starts the evolution of their thoughts and emotions, and their thinking begins to elevate. They learn from their experience and they utilize it as a stepping stone to elevate their thoughts and emotions to the next level. They continue to utilize the creative process and they continue to seek the guidance of their subconscious mind that is One with God.

We cannot continue to allow conditions, circumstances, and surroundings to obstruct the elevation of our thoughts and emotions. We must change our thought process and learn to grow from every experience of our lives that we encounter. We will never reach our full potential in life without elevating our thoughts and emotions. That is why I understand what the Apostle Paul means when he states, *"When I was a child, I spoke as a child, I understood as a child, I thought as a child; but when I became a man, I put away childish things." -1Corinthians 13:11*, It is through the maturity and growth of our minds that the real evolution of our lives take place. When our thoughts remain idle, we continue to speak, see, act, and think from a child's point of view.

It is through the elevation of our thoughts that we start to comprehend life experiences and learn from them. When we begin to understand the true power of our thoughts and the true meaning of being created in the image and likeness of God. It is then that we will start to put away our childish ways of thinking for the necessary progression of our lives. It is then that we will stop complaining about our lives, stop blaming others for our lives, and start taking responsibility for our lives. It is then that we will stop looking for the right way to do the wrong things and start doing the right things the right way. It is then that we will begin to understand that failure is a perception of our thoughts, because *"all things work together for good to those who love God." -Romans 8:28* So, every experience is looked upon as an experience to grow and evolve from.

As we continue to grow and evolve through our thoughts and emotions, we must learn from the lessons our lives are teaching us at that very moment. When we learn from these lessons, that particular life lesson becomes our past, and it makes room for other life lessons to take place. It is our comprehension of these life lessons, and how we respond to them that determines the evolution of our thoughts. We either learn from the lessons and elevate our thoughts or learn nothing and remain idle. It is your inner thoughts and emotions that produces your outer conditions, circumstances, and surroundings. We are all creators of our lives and it is through the evolution of our thoughts and emotions, that our lives will begin to change.

Our lives will always be in harmonious agreement with our inner state. It is through the evolution of our thoughts and emotions that we will be able to reach, achieve, or conquer the measure of success we desire for our lives. The evolution of our thoughts is derived through our subconscious mind that is One with God, its Source. It is the seeking of this guidance that our thoughts are elevated. When we seek guidance, our thoughts are brought up to a higher level, because it is our thoughts conforming to the thoughts of God. *"For my thoughts are not your thoughts, neither are your ways my ways," declares the LORD. "As the heavens are higher than the earth, so are my ways higher than your ways and my thoughts than your thoughts." -Isaiah 55:8-9*

THE UTILIZATION OF WILL POWER

SPIRIT CREATES BY SELF-CONTEMPLATION; THEREFORE, WHAT IT CONTEMPLATES ITSELF AS BEING, THAT IT BECOMES. YOU ARE INDIVIDUALIZED SPIRIT; THEREFORE, WHAT YOU CONTEMPLATE AS THE LAW OF YOUR BEING BECOMES THE LAW OF YOUR BEING

-THOMAS TROWARD

THE UTILIZATION OF WILL POWER

When discussing the utilization of will power, I would first like to define a couple of words. The word will mean mental powers manifested as wishing, choosing, desiring, or intending. The power of control over one's actions or emotions. The word will power means energetic determination. Our will is very important and should not be taken lightly in the utilization of the creative process. But many people seem to believe that the utilization of our subconscious mind is caused by will power. They believe will power to be the source of the creative power. This is not true.

Now I do not discount the fact that will power can develop certain superficial results, but just like any other method of force it suffers from the absence of lasting natural growth. Once the force is gone the results diminishes because the results are shallow and not of natural evolution. We should not make the mistake of believing and accrediting ourselves or will power as the creative power. The fact remains that we ourselves never created anything. Anything ever contributed to man as his creation is the unification of materials that already existed. God is the only Source of this creative power. Therefore, we cannot create what has created us.

But it is the specialization of this power that allows us to utilize it for the purpose of our creation. Our role is to be distributors of this power. Now the utilization of will power is important. Our will power should be used to choose and control our thoughts and emotions towards the positive direction of creation. It is the exerting of our will to maintain our focus on positive thoughts and positive emotions for the productivity and creation of our desires.

Using our will to maintain this positive focus tells our conscious mind to impress our positive thoughts, ideas, and desires onto our subconscious mind, it is the initial joining of Will's coming together.

By trusting the Source of the creative power of our subconscious mind, our will moves into the Will of God. When our will moves into the Will of God we follow Its guidance, because It is of Infinite Intelligence. It is the Supreme Mind, united as One with our subconscious mind. Our will is then elevated to Its level, because God's Will is Supreme over all things, therefore It could never lower Itself to our will. It can only elevate our will higher to align it into harmonious agreement with It. This is the functioning of our will when we seek the guidance of the Will of God. We are to utilize our will to direct and control thought and emotion in a positive direction for the benefit of our lives. It is the training of our will to maintain positive thoughts and emotions, and the transferring of our will from a lower level to a higher level of God's Will, that we receive the enduring and pleasurable results of our lives that we desire.

What we must comprehend is, what we do by our own will is our own deed or act. But what we do without the consent of our own will is not our deed or act. It is the deed or act of the power by which our will has submitted to and has been dominated by. Now nothing can take over our will unless we allow it to do so. So, when we seek the Will of God we willingly give up our will for the guidance of His Will.

The strengthening of our will is important, we must develop an intelligent method of concentration for the guarding and directing of our thoughts and emotions into a positive flow of creation for our lives. When I speak of this method of concentration I am not talking about a vigorous effort that drains the mind and body due to stress and tension. I am talking about a method of concentration that shuts out all negative thoughts and emotions, because we trust, recognize, and acknowledge the Source of our subconscious mind and is certain that our thoughts, ideas, and desires will be accomplished. Now the question may be asked, why God did not create us so that we would not have negative thoughts or thoughts that are not productive?

What we must understand is, for God to do this would be a contradiction of our existence. God is the Creator of all. Our thoughts and will are totally free. It is through our perception that we determine what is good, bad, positive, or negative, this is our choice. The power to choose is the authority and freedom God has given to the individual, our individuality. To choose our thoughts for us would eliminate our individuality. It is through our individuality that the Spirit wants to enjoy and experience life. For God to have individuality would be to limit Himself. But it is through the specialization of the Law of our Being that enables the Spirit to enjoy and experience life through us. We are free to utilize our power of individuality which is limitless, but we must accept the consequences of our thoughts. This is the Law of our Being, we are what we think.

Most people misunderstand this and believe they can force their will on the Law of our Being. Our will is not the creative power. It is the power of thought that is the creative cause. The function of the will is to keep our thoughts and emotions in the right direction, which will be established by enlightened thinking. Thoughts create ideas and they are the seeds that will produce the fruit of its kind. The cause and effect of our lives. The ideas created through our thoughts gives direction to the functioning of the Law of our Being.

The direction can be constructively or destructively. The Law works positively or negatively as to the thought it represents.

The will power can be used to hold together a true or inverted thought, because we believe the force of our will is enough, and it can hold down all opposition. We mistakenly believe that we are the creators of the creative power. But the fundamental principle of creative power is Oneness with God. The idea of using the force and power of our will for creativity is an inverted thought. It disrupts the function of the role we are to play, to form the wholeness of the creative order. Therefore, eliminating the growth and elevation of our own individuality, so instead of evolving we remain idle or regress. It is the mistaken conception of our role in the Creative Order that leads us to invert it.

Exerting will power may work for a while, but because it is in conflict with the power it is seeking to use, it fails. You cannot sow seeds of one kind of fruit and receive another. What we must undoubtedly understand is, it is the consciousness of our Oneness with God that is the great secret of creativity for our lives. We must truly comprehend the functioning of our will to fully utilize its power for the productiveness of our lives.

LOVE, FAITH, AND HOPE

LOVE IS PATIENT, LOVE IS KIND. IT DOES NOT ENVY, IT DOES NOT BOAST, IT IS NOT PROUD. IT DOES NOT DISHONOR OTHERS, IT IS NOT SELF-SEEKING, IT IS NOT EASILY ANGERED, IT KEEPS NO RECORD OF WRONG. LOVE DOES NOT DELIGHT IN EVIL BUT REJOICES WITH THE TRUTH. IT ALWAYS PROTECTS, ALWAYS TRUST, ALWAYS HOPES, ALWAYS PERSERVERS. LOVE NEVER FAILS.

-1CORINTHIANS 13:4-8

LOVE, FAITH, AND HOPE

I would like to address each of these inner qualities of love, faith, and hope individually before concisely addressing them together. When I think about the word love, words such as God, affection, devotion, loyalty, infatuation, and desire come to mind. The word love means, a strong affection for or attachment to another person based on regard or shared experiences or interest: A feeling of kindness or brotherhood toward others.

Love is the indispensable and inherent property that characterizes and identifies our existence. It is the nature of our Being. For most of us love defines our purpose. It is because of the love we have for our children, our spouses, and our families, that we put our concerns and needs second and theirs first. When love is real and true, it becomes much more than just a feeling, it becomes an action. *"For God so loved the world that He gave His only begotten Son, that whoever believes in Him should not perish but have everlasting life." -John 3:16*

For the love we have for our families, we sacrifice our lives, for the enrichment and enhancement of theirs. Everything we do is to better their lives, putting our love into action. Love inspirits every quality about us. Love strengthens your faith and fortifies hope. When love becomes the motivation for your purpose, it propels the creative power of your subconscious mind into motion. Love impels your mind and entices the creative power of your thoughts and ideas, mobilizing your imagination.

Love is giving and never withholds. It helps you to rid your thoughts of lack. Because you give freely, honestly, and willingly, and you attract more love back into your life. Love is never vindictive, but forgiving, and it keeps your motives, emotions, and purpose in perspective. Understanding who you are, and who's you are, helps you to acknowledge God's love for you. It is the recognition of this love that reinforces your faith and hope in the creative power of your thoughts, ideas, and your subconscious mind.

"Now faith is the substance of things hoped for, the evidence of things not seen." -Hebrews 11:1, When I think of the word faith, words such as belief, trust, confidence, and hope come to mind. The word faith means, confident belief in the truth, value, or trustworthiness of a person, idea, or thing: Belief not based on logical proof or material evidence. For me faith is a gift of God. It was stored inside of us when He created us. It is the exercising of our faith, that puts God's love into action for the betterment of our lives.

It is through the exercising of our faith in God that clears the lines of communication for us to receive the guidance of God's Will or The Will of God. When we do not have faith or lack faith in God we exercise our free will. This distorts the lines of communication between us and God. When we exercise our free will, we make our own choices and do not seek guidance from God. When we have faith, we trust God's guidance and move into His Will. We understand that we are not the Source, and that it is Him.

Our subconscious mind is our line of communication with God. When we express what we want through our thoughts, our subconscious mind receives our thoughts, and create ways to materialize those thoughts for the enjoyment of the Spirit that dwells in us to enjoy and experience life. It is with God that our faith rest, and because we believe in Him, we believe in the creative power of our subconscious mind, because they are One. So, we already possess this power and do not need to acquire it.

Our faith grows and strengthens the more we use it. It is through our faith that we trust the guidance of our inner thoughts and ideas. It is through our faith that we trust the creative power of our subconscious mind. It is our faith that allows us to stay out of our own way. When you have faith, you know your desires will come true.

"We have this hope as an anchor for the soul, firm and secure." -Hebrews 6:19, When I think of the word hope words such as trust, confidence, faith, desire, and expect comes to mind. The word hope means to wish for something with expectation of its fulfilment: To look forward to with confidence or expectation. For me hope is an inner quality to believe in yourself. Hope invigorates your faith and belief in the things you desire. What I mean by that is, you do not just wish for something, you expect it.

Hope uplifts our self-confidence in our abilities, our inner thoughts, and our ideas. Hope gives us the courage to follow our intuitions and ambitions. It makes us open-minded and receptive to the inner wisdom of our subconscious mind, allowing God to work wonders into our lives, because we expect our desires to come true. Maintaining a positive attitude and encouraging the spirit of others helps us to exhilarate our hope each day. Hope is within the depths of the soul of every person. It gives inspiration and motivation. It is hope that keeps us moving forward, knowing our thoughts will bear the fruit of the seeds we have planted.

When we look at love, faith, and hope at first glance we might view them all as emotions, or positive attributes that influences a positive attitude. But while love is described as a feeling, I believe it to be so much more. I believe God is Love. Wherever love is exposed, God is revealed. The Spirit of God dwells in all of us, so that means the Spirit of

Love dwells in us at all times. *"Do you not believe that I am in the Father, and the Father in Me? The words that I speak to you I do not speak on My own authority; but the Father who dwells in Me does the works." -John 14:10*

When we acknowledge our essence of being whole, and that is Oneness with The Creator. We allow the Love of God that shines in us to shine through us, touching the lives of everyone that encounters us. It is the performance of this love being exalted in the soul, that impels us to sacrifice our lives for others. Because authentic love is giving. So, when the Spirit of Love works through us, which is God working through us, we can accomplish anything, making the lives of everyone around us better.

Not to devalue the importance of faith and hope, because they are both inner qualities of the soul. But I put love in a class all by itself. Love, faith, and hope are motivating and assuring. They permit spiritual growth and maturity in joy and happiness, which makes them the best positive attributes for accomplishing our desires. Love, faith, and hope inspires us and gives us power. Their power uplifts and impels us to enrich and enhance the lives of other. Their power shines from within us, touching the souls of the people we meet. Love, faith, and hope eliminates all negative emotions. Fear, doubt, jealousy, and anger cannot exist wherever there is Love, Faith, and Hope! *"And now these three remain: faith, hope, and love. But the greatest of these is love." -1Corinthians 13:13*

CREATING GENERATIONAL BLESSINGS

DO NOT FOLLOW WHERE THE PATH MAY LEAD. GO INSTEAD, WHERE THERE IS NO PATH AND LEAVE A TRAIL.

-RALPH WALDO EMERSON

CREATING GENERATIONAL BLESSINGS

"A good man leaves an inheritance to his children's children, but the wealth of the sinner is stored up for the righteous." -Proverbs 13:22

Most of us was born into poverty. We have been poor our entire lives. Those of us that so call make it out of the hood still find ourselves just a few missed paychecks away from being back there living with our parents. We have been living generation after generation in poverty. The only things most of us have experienced in life is the struggles and emotional stress of committing fraud, selling drugs, doing drugs, going to prison, visiting a parent or relative in prison, having children at an early age, being on welfare, not having any money, not have a job, raising children on our own, stealing, robbing, having low self-esteem, having no self-esteem, having no confidence, no education, being full of hate, anger, fear, doubt, anxiety, etc., etc., the list goes on and on.

I hope this sounds harsh, outrageous, and cruel, because the harshest, outrageous, and cruelest thing about all of this is, we pass these generational curses on to our children with no hope in sight. We teach them that the only way out is to finish school, get a high school diploma or college degree, and find a job. We tell them to do the things tradition have told us to do. Now please do not misunderstand me. I firmly believe in education. I believe you should be educated in whatever field of work or expertise you choose to be in.

I think education and working hard, or hard work is the backbone of this country. It is what the poor and middle class have been doing our entire lives, generation after generation, "working hard." What I am trying to do with this book is share some information, give some motivation, and instill some inspiration and get you to understand that you no longer have to settle for being the backbone of this country. By utilizing your creative thoughts and ideas you have the ability to be the brains of this country.

Now, whichever one you choose is fine, it is your choice. I am just here to inform you that you have a choice. You can be the backbone or the brains. Let's examine the two. The word backbone means, the vertebrate spine or spinal column: A main support or sustaining factor: strength of character. Now, the word brain means, the part of the central nervous system in the vertebrate cranium that is responsible for interpretation of sensory impulses, coordination and control of bodily activities, and exercise of emotion and thought: A functionally similar portion of the invertebrate nervous system: Intellectual capacity: A highly intelligent person.

Now that you have the meaning of these words, I believe I am justified in saying this. The brain controls the backbone and is responsible for its functioning. A person is still able to function without a backbone. We also have animals that are invertebrates (lacking a backbone or spinal column). But no human or animal can function without a brain. Computers and automation systems may limit and replace the backbone of this country, but this country will never function or operate without it's brain.

I am not here to minimize, discredit, or take away from the importance of education or hard work. I believe in, and appreciate the value of importance, they both add to a person's intellect and character 100%. But here is where we limit ourselves with them. Now education is very necessary, but people go through years of school, get all kinds of degrees, just to find themselves working their entire lives for someone else. So, what this tells me is, going to school and getting a degree of whatever kind, let's the employer, the community, and society know that you have the capability to learn and comprehend the information in a particular field. You are able to follow instructions. But it does not mean you know how to create wealth. It does not mean you can create financial freedom for yourself.

Most people get these degrees, find a good paying job and is still unhappy. For some, they have hit a plateau and come to realize they will not be experiencing any further growth within the company they have been working for. For others, they are so stuck in the lines of tradition, that they lack the confidence and faith to follow their heart desires. I know of numerous people that have degrees and find themselves working in a field that has nothing to do with their degree or field of expertise and they are not happy. They go to work every day dreading what they do for a living. We have lost our ability to think for ourselves, and therefore do not believe in ourselves. We are unable to march to the beat of our own drum, because it sounds so unfamiliar to us.

If you have a degree in a specialize field, your degree should add value and instill confidence to your creative thoughts and ideas. You should not just settle for working a dead-end job for someone else. By completing a degree, you have already proven that you have the capability to comprehend a particular field. You just need to strengthen your faith in the entrepreneurial spirit of your subconscious mind. If you are making millions of dollars for someone else, imagine what you can do for yourself. You just need to believe in the creative process and understand, you have power in your thoughts.

The same can be said for the person who do not have a degree. You have been doing what you do for so long, that you have mastered your craft. You have built someone else's business with your ideas. The business has your fingerprints all over it. The problem is, you do not get paid for your ideas, you get paid for your work. You put in massive hours and you are barely making enough money to get by.

Now some people may not agree with me, but you will never receive the monetary value, appreciation, and proper recognition for your ideas until you are doing them for the benefit of your own business. Your creative thoughts and ideas are limitless and priceless. Your children's children should be the beneficiaries of your creative thoughts and ideas, and that is what makes them priceless. Whether we have a college degree or not, we have the capabilities within our thoughts and ideas to begin creating generational blessings for our children.

"Train up a child the way he should go, and when he is old he will not depart from it." -Proverbs 22:6, Children are very impressionable, they are easily influenced. I believe we must present ourselves as an example to our children by utilizing our creative thoughts and ideas to create wealth. We must start encouraging them to think for themselves and to follow their dreams, but we need to lead by example.

When a child sees the entrepreneurial spirit of their parents or parent on display it makes them want to follow that example. It gives them the mind set to say, "I want my own business, just like my parents owned their own business." They know it is possible because they have seen it done by you. So, they begin to develop the beliefs of "I can," "I will," and "I am able," because "you did." The creation of wealth becomes achievable and attainable to them.

Wealth is a product of the mind. I believe we must begin to change our habitual thoughts and direct our purpose for living to the creation of generational blessings for our children. We must begin to teach them to be the brains of this country and not just the backbone. Now there is nothing wrong with being the backbone, and I respect the fact that not everyone wants to explore their entrepreneurial spirit. They are happy and content with working their job. Being your own boss, controlling your own destiny, and creating financial freedom for yourself is not for everyone. But if you are open-minded and receptive to this message, then I am talking to you when I say, you should strive for being the brains of this country instead of the backbone. I mean why be Robin, when you have a choice to be Batman. Now, being Robin is cool, but know you have a choice.

If we are going to rid ourselves from these chains of poverty, these chains of tradition, these chains of conformity, we must begin to utilize the creative power of our subconscious mind. We have the brain power, the thought power, to create ideas and live the life we want. But we continue to teach our children how to follow tradition and not think for themselves. Allowing generational curses to continue affecting their lives. If we are poor or have a life of poverty we teach them that there is nothing better. We teach them a life of lack, a life of hopelessness. We condition them to blame and justify their behavior. We teach them that the world is against them. Teaching them not to take responsibility for their choices.

If we are fortunate enough to make it to college, we teach them to go to school, get married and have children. We teach them that if you find a decent job hold on to it and be happy you got a job. Teaching them to be content. We teach them everything about life that we know, but we do not teach them how to think for themselves. We do not teach them how to use their thoughts, ideas, mental images, and desires to create a life of abundance. But I guess we cannot teach them what we ourselves do not know.

You can begin to teach your children the things you are learning in this book. We can begin to teach them about the power of their thoughts, emotions, and beliefs. We can teach them about the power they have within themselves. We can teach them about their conscious and subconscious mind, and how the two works together. We can teach them how to utilize their subconscious mind and the creative process, such as how to create, visualize, and believe. We can teach them how to create wealth and the importance of maintaining a positive emotional state.

We can teach them about the power of forgiveness and our ability to create. We can teach them the importance of love, faith, and hope, as well as the importance of being thankful, showing gratitude, and encouraging others. But most importantly, teach them about the Love of God, who is the Source of the creation of our thoughts and ideas. Teach them that we have the power to create, but He is The Creator. Teach them to teach their children to pursue their inner thoughts and ideas. What are the benefits of your struggles, if your children go through the same struggles you went through. Our struggles and sacrifices should be for the enhancement and enrichment of their lives.

It is changing our way of thinking and our habitual thoughts toward a positive direction, that is going to create the generational blessings that we desire for our children and their children. We must instill in our children, that they have the ability to create the life they want for themselves.

Utilizing what we learn and passing it on to our children is a start. Our children are so impressionable and being a positive example for them can change their lives and generations after them forever. Generational curses have been haunting our families for decades. We now have the opportunity to change those generational curses into generational blessings, and we do it by utilizing our creative thoughts and ideas.

Our ignorance is no longer an excuse. God has given each of us supreme authority through our thoughts. Generational blessings are just thoughts and ideas away. So, begin right now to utilize the creative power of your subconscious mind and begin to change not just your life, but the lives of your future generations. They say if you give a man a fish he eats for a day, but if you teach him to fish he eats for a life time. Teach your children how to fish, teach them how to flip the switch of the creative power of their subconscious mind. *"Children's children are a crown to the aged, and parents are the pride of their children." - Proverbs 17:6*

LET ME SAY THIS

You have the power in your thoughts to be or do whatever you desire and live the lifestyle that you want. It all starts with how you treat others and the way you feel about yourself. Being thankful, showing gratitude, and encouraging others is a way you can begin to uplift the spirit, confidence, and emotions of others. In doing so you begin to uplift your own spirit, confidence, and emotions. Instead of looking at things from a negative perspective, you start to look at things from a positive perspective. You become more open-minded to your circumstances and learn from them. Your attitude changes and you feel good about the things and people in your life, understanding that things could be worst, but you are thankful for what they are.

Our life is about growth, so the more things you start to be thankful for the more things start to change in your life. Creating better conditions, circumstances, and surroundings for you to be thankful for. Being thankful is a great quality to have when developing a positive attitude. We must start being thankful for the things we have now. Start focusing on what you want and stop focusing on what you do not want.

Showing gratitude is a form of expression to reveal to someone that you are thankful for them and the things they do. Simple gestures, such as leaving a spouse a thank you note, telling them how thankful you are for the things they do, how much you love them, and how lucky you are to have them in your life. It expresses to them that you treasure your relationship with them, and that you acknowledge the things that they do. This simple token of appreciation is priceless to someone who might have been having a bad day, feeling depressed, or lacking self-esteem.

Uplifting the spirit of others, helps you to maintain positive emotions and a positive attitude. It is a form of encouraging others as well. Being there for a child's game or recital means a great deal to them. Telling them how great of a job they did, and how proud you are of them, strengthens and validates the confidence they already have within. Uplifting a child's spirit when they fail or lose at something, teaches them that failing is not failure, and it is not the end. It helps them to restore the confidence they may have lost. Being there for a friend or neighbor when tragedy strikes, letting them know that this too shall pass and that you will be there for them. It is extraordinary qualities such as these that allows you to feel good about yourself, while helping others.

Feeling good about yourself puts you in a desirable and positive emotional state. Feeling good is important in life and the creative process of your subconscious mind. It puts you in an agreeable and pleasant disposition aligning you into one accord with your creative thoughts and ideas. Feeling good keeps your emotions positive and under control. When you feel good, that means your thoughts are good. Your emotions will always tell you what you are thinking in the aspect of negative or positive, bad, or good. Feeling good strengthens your self-confidence, your beliefs, your abilities, and your faith. When you maintain feeling good, having a positive attitude, and being in a positive emotional state, your habitual thinking becomes constructive and positive. You begin to flip the switch of the creative power of your subconscious mind, from negative thoughts to positive thoughts.

We must understand that wanting something good for ourselves but feeling bad all the time, do not work together. We must begin to feel good about our lives now and focus our habitual thoughts on the way we want our lives to be right now. We must leave our past behind us and utilize the power of forgiveness. Releasing negative emotions such as resentment, bitterness, and self-pity. Feeling good builds confidence, worthiness, and deservedness. Strengthening our trust in the abilities of our subconscious mind.

We trust our subconscious mind, because we have faith in its Source, God. Trusting our subconscious mind, it's ability, and power can lead to the creation of spiritual, mental, and financial freedom. We have to trust the guidance of our subconscious mind and we must control our habitual thoughts. Our thoughts and ideas need to remain focused on the wealth, abundance, and success we want for our lives. We must keep our thoughts, ideas, mental images, and desires guarded and protected. We cannot allow the discouragement of others about our ideas, thoughts, mental images, and desires to influence our trust in our subconscious mind.

We must be aware of the crabs in a bucket syndrome or mentality that we or others may have and understand that everyone is not going to believe in us or want to see us succeed. Their minds are still flooded with fear, hatred, anger, and doubt, also their happiness is in our failures. So, we need to keep our thoughts, ideas, mental images, and desires in the incubator of our mind until they are ready to breathe life. We must exercise our spirit, emotions, and mind to build up the trust and confidence we need to have in the abilities of our subconscious mind. By continuing to utilize the creative process and ideas in this book, we will strengthen our trust in our subconscious mind. Allowing us to flex our muscles of faith and belief toward any negative criticism we may receive.

Having a positive attitude will help us to overcome any negative comments, opinions, or remarks by our critics or them crabs in a bucket I mentioned earlier. Having a positive attitude allows you to be guided by the creative power of your subconscious mind toward the circumstances that will help you materialize your thoughts, ideas, and desires. It guides you in executing your creative plan for wealth and success. A positive attitude is an attractive personality trait. It can open doors for you and help you to achieve your desires quicker. It attracts wealth, health, and success. Having a positive attitude shows others that you do not allow your failures, conditions, and misfortunes to determine who you are. We must surround ourselves with people that resembles the same attitude and success we desire to develop.

Auto suggestion is no option for a person looking to maintain a positive attitude. Our mind can be so easy distracted, so we must keep our habitual thoughts focused on the life we want to have for ourselves. When you have a positive attitude you are thankful, you show gratitude, and you encourage others. A positive attitude allows you to forgive others, as well as yourself. You are able to release any hatred, resentment, or self-pity you may be holding onto inside.

This permits you to focus your energy toward your positive thoughts and ideas. By having a positive attitude, you are open-minded, and you accept people for who they are. You do not engage in conversations of gossip or hatred of others. Having a positive attitude is constructive, attractive, promotes growth, and maturity. It gives you the confidence and belief that you are capable of accomplishing anything. It is our positive attitude and the power of our thoughts that initiates the creation of our ideas.

This world was created by the thoughts of God. We have the ability to originate and create our own ideas. We have been given the power to affect our conditions, circumstances, and surroundings through our thoughts. The one thing that is different about any human being is that we can think for ourselves. We have the capacity to create our own thoughts and ideas. We have been given supreme authority over our thoughts to create ideas, that will be materialized and make a difference in this world.

Our thoughts have mystical powers, they solve, controls, directs and conquers. You and only you have the power to control your thoughts and emotions. Do not allow your negative conditions or the negative thoughts and emotions of others to influence you. You have all the answers and all the power you need within, to create generational blessings and to live the life you envision for yourself.

BONUS

A MESSAGE FROM THE AUTHOR

YOU ARE TODAY WHERE YOUR THOUGHTS HAVE BROUGHT YOU; YOU WILL BE TOMORROW WHERE YOUR THOUGHTS TAKE YOU.

-JAMES ALLEN

A MESSAGE FROM THE AUTHOR

When I first decided to write this, I tried to figure out what topics should I discuss, what was it I wanted to talk about, and how should I express it. I spent several days trying to figure out my purpose for writing these pages. I came to one inspiring decision. You the readers are my purpose for these writings. I decided to write what flowed from my mind and soul. These writings are an expression of my thoughts. To tame them into a certain order or proper format will be doing them and injustice. So, I allowed them to flow from within me, just as a child's genuine love flows from his or her soul.

A child's love is genuine just as his or her creative thoughts and ideas are. It is not until the contamination of tradition and conformity by man, that they start to believe that, them thinking outside of the box is wrong. A child's thoughts and ideas are pure, true, and honest. If you ask them a question, they will give you a pure, true, and honest answer. Children have a trusting attitude. They trust the adults they depend on to guide them and direct them. They listen to their inner voice inside. Children are trusting, receptive, and open-minded. That is why I get a firm understanding from the Bible when *Luke 18:17* states *"Truly I tell you anyone who will not receive the kingdom of God like a little child will never enter it."*

When I talk about a child being trusting, receptive, and open-minded I am referring to their positive outlook on life. They have an authentic faith. Their faith is pure, true, and honest. They do not need a complete intellectual understanding of everything that functions in this world. They do not need a completed understanding of all the mysteries of the universe. Their love for us, belief in who we are, and trust in our guidance is enough for them. Children have the right attitude when it comes to having faith.

Because having "childlike faith" is contrary to having "I must see it now faith". Most of us adults exemplify "I must see it now faith." There is no childlike expression of trust when we seek the guidance of God. We do not listen to our own thoughts and ideas. We give no acknowledgement to that inner voice within our being that gives us the answers and guidance we seek. We would rather listen to the outer voices of others who influences us with their opinions and experiences, instead of listening to our own thoughts and ideas, our own truth.

We continue to let our Bachelor's, Master's, and Doctorate's degrees of education, along with our sophisticated reasoning deter us away from what is true for us and to us. Our thoughts have been obstructed by our life experiences, letting our past hinder us from hearing the inner voice of God that dwells within us. We must begin to have true faith in that inner voice of our mind, our thoughts, and our ideas. We must reestablish that "childlike faith" of creativity that allows us to be original, and not be afraid of our own thoughts and ideas. But follow them, because they come from us, the inner depths of our soul guided by God, designed for us to share with the world. It is for this reason I will not tame, domesticate, or subdue my thoughts but let them be as adventurous as they were designed to be.

It is sometimes difficult to put away your past experiences, but you should not allow your past to dictate your future or current experiences. "Let your past be a learning experience and not a confirming experience." Meaning, just because someone broke your heart, betrayed your trust, or you have failed at something in the past, do not mean you should not love again, trust again or try again for the rest of your life. You need to watch who you love and trust and educate yourself on what you try. But also understand that you are worthy and deserving to have loving and trustworthy people in your life, and you should continue to follow your dreams, because failing is not failure.

I am all for getting your degree. In fact, I encourage my daughters to get as much education for themselves that is possible. But I also teach them to follow their dreams. I understand that school is not for everyone, and just because someone chooses a different route in life other than the traditional route of school, do not make them a failure and do not mean they will be a failure. Maybe the entrepreneurial spirit within them goes far beyond anything I can see or imagine. But who am I to deprive or discourage them from their truth.

I believe we must start to change our perceptions of the way we view situations and begin to change our thought process and attitude toward life. We need to become more trusting, receptive, and open-minded about our life experiences and begin to develop a positive outlook and attitude about ourselves and our lives. We seem to believe that if we get our life in order we will begin to change the way we think or see things. I do not believe that to be true. I believe we need to get our thoughts in order, change the way we think, and our lives will begin to change. I believe that when we change the way we think, we will begin to change our lives. Because we will begin to see things from a different point of view. We begin to see the glass as half full, instead of half empty.

Everything in this world started with a thought and will continue to evolve with a thought. When I think about the things that are going on in the world today. We base our social opinions on these issues according to how we view them. Our feelings are involved on these issues according to how we view them. How we view them is based on our thought process, meaning what we think about the issue.

Let's look at drugs and alcohol. Many people have based their beliefs that the selling and use of drugs and alcohol has destroyed the black communities and households. Now being a Black or African American male and have grown up in the ghettos or streets of Chicago, one might think I would agree with this, but I do not. Maybe in the past I may have agreed with that statement, but knowing and believing the things I understand now, I would have to take the stance of disagreement on that statement. I am a firm believer in the power of our thoughts, our subconscious mind, and how we view and deal with adversity. I believe in our inherent power to create conditions, circumstances, and surroundings with the creative power of our thoughts and ideas through our habitual thinking.

But back to the subject of drugs and alcohol that has destroyed the black communities and households. Now I know some people that drink alcohol, some that smoke marijuana, and some that do both. These people function fine in society and deal with their problems or adversity well. Now I also know some people that drink alcohol, some that smoke marijuana, and some that do both. These people do not deal with their problems or adversity so well. In fact, they let the drinking and smoking consume them and the functioning of their lives.

But I believe to justify and blame the selling and use of drugs and alcohol as the reason for the problem is to camouflage and cover up the real issues that needs to be addressed. Because when we camouflage and cover them up, the problem and issues are still there. The thing I look at first is why is the person doing drugs or alcohol. The person turns to drugs and alcohol to deal with or cover up their problems. They let thoughts of fear, doubt, anger, frustration, and hopelessness consume their every thought. They become afraid to face the consequences of the decisions they have made or must make.

So, when you have one group that can and another group that cannot, it is hard to blame it on the drugs and alcohol. In fact, I would even say it is not the drugs and alcohol, but it is the thoughts and emotions of the individual. The drugs and alcohol are not the core of the problem, it is the thoughts of the person, that is the core of the problem. It is the thoughts of the person that lead them to do drugs or alcohol. If we are taught to think differently, control our emotions, and face the consequences of our decisions, then drugs and alcohol do not become an option that we choose. When we use drugs and alcohol to deal with our problems we are only finding a scapegoat to blame and justify the decisions we make.

Because when you are on drugs and alcohol your thinking and thoughts are irrational. Which mean your thoughts are not endowed with reason or understanding. Your thoughts lack usual or normal mental clarity or coherence. So, I must disagree with the statement that drugs and alcohol have destroyed my communities and households. When the reality of it is, our thoughts, our way of thinking and our emotional inability to deal with and solve the problems that we are faced with have destroyed the black communities and households.

The use of drugs and alcohol is a symptom of the underlying problem, just like poverty, black on black violence, and single parent homes. These symptoms are an indication that something is wrong but getting rid of the symptom does not mean that the problem is gone. No more than getting rid of a bad cough means you no longer have the flu. You may have temporarily stopped coughing, but the flu is still there. We must get rid of the viruses of our mind that is within our habitual thinking, and all the symptoms will begin to disappear.

We begin this process by changing our thoughts. We must begin to change the way we think about ourselves, our communities, and our households. We must reeducate and refine the thinking of our very existence in the world today. As a black man in my community, I must acknowledge and take responsibility for my actions. I have been an embarrassment and a disappointment to my family and my community. I have contributed to the stereotypes of the black males. I have been divorced, incarcerated, and my children has been raised with their parents in two separate homes.

Now, if the direction of my focus continues to be on my failures to my community, family, and the fact that I am a convicted felon. Then according to society my future, my children's future, and my community's future has already been predicted. I find this to be false and untrue in every sense of its meaning. I believe the path to addressing or overcoming a situation, is acknowledging, and accepting responsibility for it. So, the first thing we must do is accept responsibility for our roles in our incarcerations, abandonment of our women, children, and communities and the relinquishment of our financial responsibilities to our women, children, and communities.

We must acknowledge how we are contributing to these stereotypes and find solutions, as to what we can do differently to help ourselves and others steer clear away from these stereotypes. We must learn to take control of our thoughts and emotions and stop letting our thoughts and emotions take control of us. We must make decisions based upon how they affect others and stop being selfish, only thinking about ourselves. We must start looking at the consequences of our actions and the decisions we make. We must also, start looking at who they affect and how they affect them. We must start taking responsibility for our actions and decisions and stop blaming others for the outcome of our lives.

We can no longer afford to take what I believe to be the easy way out. Because it is this easy way out that is costing our families, communities, and generations to come the most important asset they need to succeed in this world and that asset is us. Our presence, our encouragement, our guidance, our financial support, and our leadership as men. We must make the conscious decision that no matter what the conditions, circumstances, or surrounding are, we will not abandon our women, children, and communities anymore. Because they are the ones that are suffering the most from our thoughts, our ideas, our thinking, our decision making, or shall I say the lack there of. It is our way of thinking that is destroying our families and communities, and the fact remains, we must change our way of thinking and begin utilizing and materializing the creative thoughts and ideas that are in our minds today, for the betterment of our future.

EACH ONE TEACH ONE!

www.ingramcontent.com/pod-product-compliance
Lightning Source LLC
Chambersburg PA
CBHW052027070526
44584CB00016B/1937